Prajapathy Molagoda
S.S.C.

A BOOK OF ENGLISH POEMS

A BOOK OF ENGLISH POEMS

GRADED FOR USE IN SCHOOLS

By J. H. JAGGER, M.A., D.Litt.

		Limp Cloth	
Introductory Part	108 pp.	1s. 3d.	

		Limp Cloth	Cloth Boards
Book One	112 pp.	1s. 3d.	1s. 6d.
Book Two	112 pp.	1s. 3d.	1s. 6d.
Book Three	160 pp.	1s. 9d.	2s. 0d.
Book Four	176 pp.	2s. 0d.	2s. 3d.

UNIVERSITY OF LONDON PRESS, Ltd.

A BOOK OF
ENGLISH POEMS

GRADED FOR USE IN SCHOOLS

BY

J. H. JAGGER, M.A., D.Litt.

PART FOUR

ILLUSTRATED BY GLADYS M. REES

NEW IMPRESSION

LONDON
UNIVERSITY OF LONDON PRESS, LTD.
10 & 11 WARWICK LANE, E.C.4
1929

FIRST PRINTED	.	.	.	*November* 1925
Reprinted	.	.	.	*December* 1927
Reprinted	.	.	.	*November* 1929

Printed in Great Britain for the UNIVERSITY OF LONDON PRESS, LTD., by HAZELL, WATSON AND VINEY, LD., London and Aylesbury.

CONTENTS

		PAGE
INTRODUCTION		ix

I

Hymn to Diana	B. Jonson	1
"All early in the April"	J. Masefield	1
Counsel to Girls	R. Herrick	3
To Althea, from Prison	R. Lovelace	4
To Lucasta, on going to the Wars	R. Lovelace	5
"You meaner beauties of the night"	Sir H. Wotton	5
The Ladies of St. James's	A. Dobson	6
"My love is like a red, red rose"	R. Burns	8
"Fear no more the heat of the sun"	W. Shakespeare	9
"Come away, come away, death"	W. Shakespeare	10
Song for Saint Cecilia's Day	J. Dryden	10
Battle Song	E. Elliott	13

II

"If all the pens that ever poets held"	C. Marlowe	15
Ode	A. O'Shaughnessy	15
On First Looking into Chapman's Homer	J. Keats	17
Lycidas	J. Milton	18
In Memoriam A. H.	M. Baring	25
On the Countess Dowager of Pembroke	W. Browne	32
Il Penseroso	J. Milton	32
Lying in the Grass	E. Gosse	37
Worldly Paradise	N. Breton	40
The Soldier	R. Brooke	41
The Volunteer	Sir H. Newbolt	42

Contents

			PAGE
23 BRUMANA	*J. E. Flecker*	.	42
24 THE LOTOS EATERS	*Lord Tennyson*		44
25 SONNET	*J. C. Squire*	.	46
26 "SOUND, SOUND THE CLARION"	*Sir W. Scott*	.	47
27 INTO BATTLE	*J. Grenfell*	.	47
28 "CHILDE ROLAND TO THE DARK TOWER CAME"	*R. Browning*	.	49
29 WATERLOO	*Lord Byron*	.	54
30 AGHADOE	*J. Todhunter*	.	57

III

31 MORNING	*E. Underhill*	.	59
32 ABT VOGLER	*R. Browning*	.	59
33 KUBLA KHAN	*S. T. Coleridge*	.	63
34 FLANNAN ISLE	*W. W. Gibson*	.	65
35 KEITH OF RAVELSTON	*S. Dobell*	.	69

IV

36 THE GARDEN	*A. Marvell*	.	73
37 THE BOWER OF BLISS	*E. Spenser*	.	75
38 "THERE IS A HILL BESIDE THE SILVER THAMES"	*R. Bridges*	.	77
39 THE BRIDGE	*J. R. Anderson*		80
40 ODE TO AUTUMN	*J. Keats*	.	82
41 TO A SKYLARK	*P. B. Shelley*	.	84
42 TO A MOUSE	*R. Burns*	.	88
43 LINES WRITTEN IN EARLY SPRING	*W. Wordsworth*	.	90
44 UPON WESTMINSTER BRIDGE, SEPTEMBER 3, 1802	*W. Wordsworth*	.	91
45 THE MUSIC OF THE SPHERES	*W. Shakespeare*	.	92

V

46 AMPHION	*Lord Tennyson*	.	93
47 THE VICAR OF BRAY	*Anonymous*	.	97
48 MACFLECKNOE	*J. Dryden*	.	99
49 THE BALLAD OF BEAU BROCADE	*A. Dobson*	.	100

Contents

vii

			PAGE
THE SOCIETY UPON THE STANISLAUS.	F. Bret Harte	.	109
DUNCAN GRAY	R. Burns	.	111
MUIOPOTMOS	E. Spenser	.	112

VI

"FULL MANY A GLORIOUS MORNING HAVE I SEEN"	W. Shakespeare	.	119
BALLADE OF GOOD COUNSEL	G. Chaucer	.	119
FREEDOM	J. Barbour	.	120
"IT IS NOT TO BE THOUGHT OF THAT THE FLOOD"	W. Wordsworth	.	121
ENGLAND AND SWITZERLAND, 1802	W. Wordsworth	.	122
"THE WORLD IS TOO MUCH WITH US"	W. Wordsworth	.	123
"MY MIND TO ME A KINGDOM IS"	Sir E. Dyer	.	123
"HE THAT OF SUCH A HEIGHT HATH BUILT HIS MIND"	S. Daniel	.	125
THE CHAMBERED NAUTILUS	O. W. Holmes	.	126
INTIMATIONS OF IMMORTALITY	W. Wordsworth	.	127
CHORUS	A. C. Swinburne	.	131
"LIKE TO THE FALLING OF A STAR"	H. King	.	133
CHARLES THE TWELFTH	S. Johnson	.	133
RECESSIONAL	R. Kipling	.	135
THE CONCLUSION	Sir W. Raleigh	.	136
"THE GLORIES OF OUR BLOOD AND STATE"	J. Shirley	.	136
UXBRIDGE ROAD	E. Underhill	.	137
ON HIS BLINDNESS	J. Milton	.	139
THE BOOK	W. Drummond	.	139
ODE IN MAY	Sir W. Watson	.	140
TO A SNOWFLAKE	F. Thompson	.	142
"NIGHT UNTO NIGHT SHOWETH KNOWLEDGE"	W. Habington	.	143

VERSE EXERCISES 145

ACKNOWLEDGMENTS OF COPYRIGHT.

For permission to print the poems named, grateful thanks are due to the following publishers, authors, and owners of copyright:

Messrs. William Heinemann, Ltd., for *In Memoriam A. H.*, from *Collected Poems*, by Mr. Maurice Baring; *Lying in the Grass*, by Sir Edmund Gosse; and *Chorus from Atalanta*, by A. C. Swinburne.

Messrs. Martin Secker, Ltd., for *Brumana*, from *Collected Poems*, by J. E. Flecker.

Messrs. Sidgwick & Jackson, Ltd., for *The Soldier*, from *Collected Poems*, by Rupert Brooke; and *The Bridge*, from *Walls and Hedges*, by Mr. J. R. Anderson.

Sir Henry Newbolt, for *The Volunteer*, from *Poems New and Old*, published by Mr. John Murray.

Mr. John Murray, for *There is a hill beside the silver Thames*, by Dr. Robert Bridges.

Mr. J. C. Squire, for *Sonnet*.

The Right Hon. the Lord Desborough, K.C.V.O., for *Into Battle*, by the late Capt. the Hon. Julian F. H. Grenfell, D.S.O., 1st Royal Dragoons.

Messrs. James B. Pinker & Son and the Authoress, for *Uxbridge Road*, by Miss Evelyn Underhill.

Messrs. Elkin Mathews, Ltd., for *Flannan Isle*, from *Fires*, by Mr. W. W. Gibson.

Mr. Humphrey Milford (Oxford University Press) and Mr. A. T. A. Dobson (for the Trustees), for *The Ballad of Beau Brocade* and *The Ladies of St. James's*, by Austin Dobson.

Mr. Rudyard Kipling, for *Recessional*, from *The Five Nations*, published by Messrs. Methuen & Co., Ltd.

Sir William Watson, for *Ode in May*.

Messrs. Burns, Oates & Washbourne, Ltd., for *To a Snowflake*, by Francis Thompson.

Mrs. Todhunter, for *Aghadoe*, by the late Dr. John Todhunter, from *The Land of Dreams*, published by the Talbot Press, Dublin.

INTRODUCTION

THE clear vision of the poet penetrates to the heart of life and of things, and he offers to us a higher truth than we ourselves can discover. He tells us what he sees, he does not wait to reason. Slowly, with painful labour, the botanist has learnt the nature of the daisy; step by step he describes its parts, the uses of those parts, how it grows, and how closely it resembles other flowers and other things. The poet beholds the daisy as a whole, he sees its meaning in a flash of inspiration, even if he sees it imperfectly, and in his writing he imparts his secret to us. Therefore, in a sense, the aim of Poetry is the same as the aim of Science; its aim is the discovery and description of truth. But the poet himself is part of the world, for it is his own vision that he gives us, and so his message has a double meaning. The true poet reveals the soul of man as well as the meaning of the world around us.

In the first section of this book are to be found lyrics, or songs, which are the purest form of poetry. Lyrical poems are expressions of some feeling, of joy, or wonder, or sorrow, and cover the whole range of human experience. Following this section is a group of narrative poems and poems on various aspects of life, which are less lyrical in tone. The third section contains nature poems. Man's appreciation of the garden in which he finds himself varies from age to age. Sometimes he scarcely seems to notice it; or, if he notices it, it is merely as a background for himself. At other times he loses himself in the contemplation of his earthly environment. Yet again, he strives to pierce through the veil held by nature before his eyes, to the spirit which stands behind it.

His restless, soaring imagination, however, cannot be confined by the actual; it seeks to voyage through "other lands and other seas," which it creates for itself; it has power to make and to unmake, and to pass the bounds of time and space. Poems of this kind compose the fourth group.

Omitting comic poems and light verse, which need no explanation here, we come finally to the highest range of poetry, where the poet is impelled to write upon solemn subjects. Many lyrics are seductive and soft, and if others, like battle-songs, brace the sinews and exalt the spirit in moments of personal or national stress, they are still poems of strong emotion. But before the deepest mysteries of existence emotion is fitly replaced by reverent contemplation, or is, at any rate, best when allied with contemplation. The most serious poems, with which the book closes, are also those which can give the keenest and loftiest pleasure.

English poetry is of famous antiquity. The earliest extant example of it is more than twelve hundred years old. During the Middle Ages the art of poetry was cultivated, and our first great poet, Geoffrey Chaucer, lived then. The latter part of the sixteenth century and the first half of the seventeenth were a time when poets of all kinds flourished—dramatists, sonneteers, writers of songs and of long narrative poems. Although, subsequently, poetry became more prosaic, another great flowering-time occurred during the lives of Keats, Byron, Shelley, and Wordsworth, at the beginning of the nineteenth century. Whether the poetry that is being written now will prove equal to what these ages have bequeathed to us is hard to decide; yet the modern poems in this book are enough to encourage a confident belief that the twentieth century will have no cause for shame in the future, while the old poems with which they are mingled come from a great body of literature the possession of which ought to fill the heart of every Englishman with a noble pride.

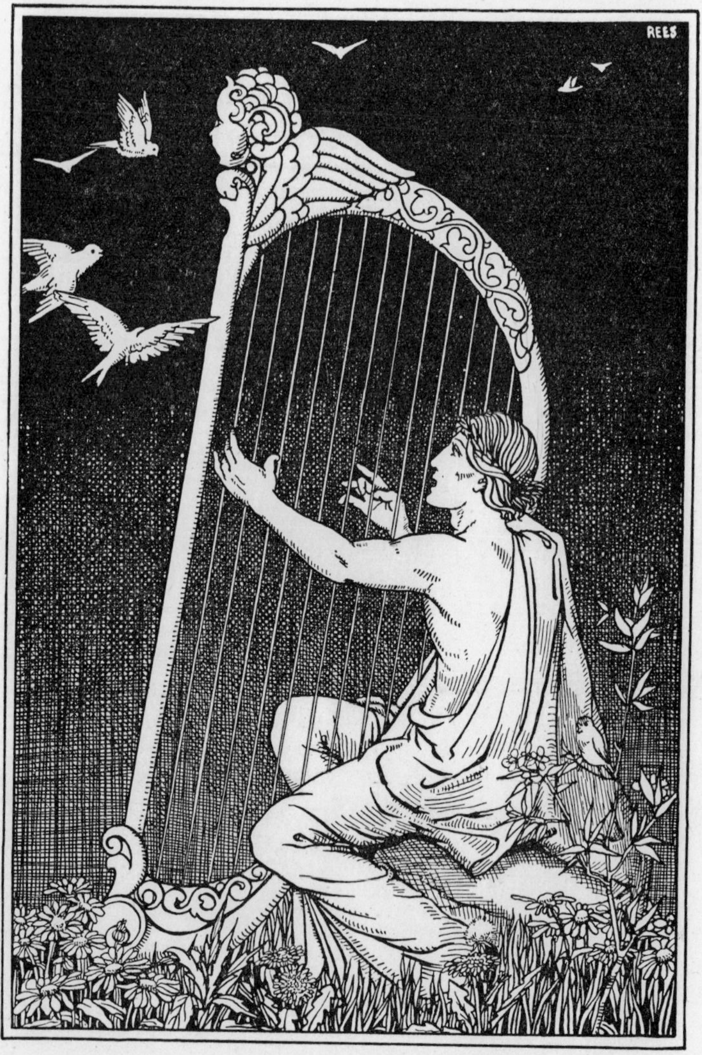
REES

A BOOK OF ENGLISH POEMS

I
HYMN TO DIANA

With surpassing skill Ben Jonson contrived to impart to his hymn to the Moon the clear, cold, white quality of moonlight. For finished grace and lucid restraint this lyric is unexcelled.

Queen and huntress, chaste and fair,
    Now the sun is laid to sleep,
Seated in thy silver chair
    State in wonted manner keep:
Hesperus entreats thy light,
Goddess excellently bright.

Earth, let not thy envious shade
    Dare itself to interpose;
Cynthia's shining orb was made
    Heaven to clear when day did close:
Bless us then with wishèd sight,
Goddess excellently bright.

Lay thy bow of pearl apart,
    And thy crystal-shining quiver;
Give unto the flying hart
    Space to breathe, how short soever:
Thou that mak'st a day of night,
Goddess excellently bright.
                  Ben Jonson.

"ALL EARLY IN THE APRIL"

All early in the April, when daylight comes at five,
I went into the garden, most glad to be alive;

The thrushes and the blackbirds were singing in the thorn,
The April flowers were singing for joy of being born.

I smelt the dewy morning come blowing through the woods,
Where all the wilding cherries do toss their snowy snoods;
I thought of the running water where sweet white violets grow.
I said: "I'll pick them for her, because she loves them so."

So in the dewy morning I turned to climb the hill
Beside the running water whose tongue is never still.
Oh, delicate green and dewy were all the budding trees;
The blue dog-violets grew there, and many primroses.

Out of the wood I wandered, but paused upon the heath
To watch, beyond the tree-tops, the wrinkled sea beneath;
Its blueness and its stillness were trembling as it lay
In the old unautumned beauty that never goes away.

. . . . .

All early in the May-time, when daylight comes at four,
We blessed the hawthorn blossom that welcomed us ashore.

"*All early in the April*"

Oh, beautiful in this living that passes like the foam
It is to go with sorrow, yet come with beauty home!

From " Enslaved," by John Masefield.

COUNSEL TO GIRLS

The figurative language of this poem and the next, which, as much as their smooth metre and musical rhymes, is the secret of their great beauty, will richly repay examination.

GATHER ye rosebuds while ye may,
    Old Time is still a-flying:
And this same flower that smiles to-day
    To-morrow will be dying.

The glorious Lamp of Heaven, the Sun,
    The higher he's a-getting,
The sooner will his race be run,
    And nearer he's to setting.

That age is best which is the first,
    When youth and blood are warmer;
But being spent, the worse, and worst
    Times still succeed the former.

Then be not coy, but use your time;
    And, while ye may, go marry:
For having lost but once your prime,
    You may for ever tarry.

Robert Herrick.

TO ALTHEA, FROM PRISON

The author of this famous song was a Cavalier poet who was imprisoned for seven weeks by order of the House of Commons. He had presented to Parliament a petition which brought upon him its severe displeasure. He did not take an active part in the Civil War, but he spent his fortune in the cause of the King and died in poverty.

When Love with unconfinèd wings
   Hovers within my gates,
And my divine Althea brings
   To whisper at the grates;
When I lie tangled in her hair
   And fettered to her eye,
The birds that wanton in the air
   Know no such liberty.

When flowing cups run swiftly round
   With no allaying Thames,
Our careless heads with roses bound,
   Our hearts with loyal flames;
When thirsty grief in wine we steep,
   When healths and draughts go free—
Fishes that tipple in the deep
   Know no such liberty.

When, like committed [1] linnets, I
   With shriller throat shall sing
The sweetness, mercy, majesty,
   And glories of my King;
When I shall voice aloud how good
   He is, how great should be,
Enlargèd winds, that curl the flood,
   Know no such liberty.

[1] Imprisoned.

To Althea, from Prison

Stone walls do not a prison make,
   Nor iron bars a cage;
Minds innocent and quiet take
   That for an hermitage;
If I have freedom in my love,
   And in my soul am free,
Angels alone, that soar above,
   Enjoy such liberty.
                    Richard Lovelace.

TO LUCASTA, ON GOING TO THE WARS

Tell me not, sweet, I am unkind,
   That from the nunnery
Of thy chaste breast and quiet mind
   To war and arms I fly.

True, a new mistress now I chase,
   The first foe in the field;
And with a stronger faith embrace
   A sword, a horse, a shield.

Yet this inconstancy is such
   As you too shall adore;
I could not love thee, dear, so much,
   Loved I not honour more.
                    Richard Lovelace.

"YOU MEANER BEAUTIES OF THE NIGHT"

You meaner beauties of the night,
   That poorly satisfy our eyes
More by your number than your light,
   You common people of the skies,
What are you when the Moon shall rise?

You curious chanters of the wood,
   That warble forth dame Nature's lays,
Thinking your passions understood
   By your weak accents, what's your praise
When Philomel her voice shall raise ?

You violets that first appear,
   By your pure purple mantles known
Like the proud virgins of the year,
   As if the spring were all your own,—
What are you, when the Rose is blown ?

So when my mistress shall be seen
   In form and beauty of her mind,
By virtue first, then choice, a Queen,
   Tell me if she was not designed
Th' eclipse and glory of her kind ?
                              Sir Henry Wotton.

THE LADIES OF ST. JAMES'S

The ladies of St. James's
   Go swinging to the play ;
Their footmen run before them,
   With a " Stand by ! clear the way ! "
But Phyllida, my Phyllida !
   She takes her buckled shoon,
When we go out a-courting
   Beneath the harvest moon.

The ladies of St. James's
   Wear satin on their backs ;
They sit all night at *Ombre*,
   With candles all of wax :

The Ladies of St. James's

But Phyllida, my Phyllida!
 She dons her russet gown,
And hastes to gather May dew
 Before the world is down.

The ladies of St. James's!
 They are so fine and fair
You'd think a box of essences
 Was broken in the air:
But Phyllida, my Phyllida!
 The breath of heath and furze,
When breezes blow at morning,
 Is not so fresh as hers.

The ladies of St. James's!
 They're painted to the eyes,
Their white it stays for ever,
 Their red it never dies:
But Phyllida, my Phyllida!
 Her colour comes and goes;
It trembles to a lily,—
 It wavers to a rose.

The ladies of St. James's!
 You scarce can understand
The half of all their speeches,
 Their phrases are so grand:
But Phyllida, my Phyllida!
 Her shy and simple words
Are clear as after rain-drops
 The music of the birds.

The ladies of St. James's!
 They have their fits and freaks;

They smile on you—for seconds ;
  They frown on you—for weeks :
But Phyllida, my Phyllida !
  Come either storm or shine,
From Shrove-tide unto Shrove-tide
  Is always true—and mine.

My Phyllida ! my Phyllida !
  I care not though they heap
The hearts of all St. James's,
  And give me all to keep ;
I care not whose the beauties
  Of all the world may be,
For Phyllida—for Phyllida
  Is all the world to me !

Austin Dobson.

"MY LOVE IS LIKE A RED, RED ROSE"

My love is like a red, red rose
  That's newly sprung in June :
My love is like a melody
  That's sweetly played in tune.

So fair art thou, my bonnie lass,
  So deep in love am I ;
And I will love thee still, my dear,
  Till all the seas gang dry.

Till all the seas gang dry, my dear,
  And the rocks melt wi' the sun ;
And I will love thee still, my dear,
  While the sands o' life shall run.

"*My Love is like a Red, Red Rose*" 9

And fare thee weel, my only love,
And fare thee weel awhile!
And I will come again, my love,
Tho' it were ten thousand mile.
Robert Burns.

"FEAR NO MORE THE HEAT OF THE SUN"

One of the characteristics of great poetry is that it contains striking and beautiful imagery. If it lacks this, neither glowing passion, nor felicitous phrases, nor music of metre will save it. In this poem all these qualities are present.

FEAR no more the heat o' the sun,
  Nor the furious winter's rages;
Thou thy worldly task hast done:
  Home art gone, and ta'en thy wages:
Golden lads and girls all must,
As chimney-sweepers, come to dust.

Fear no more the frown o' the great,
  Thou art past the tyrant's stroke;
Care no more to clothe and eat;
  To thee the reed is as the oak:
The sceptre, learning, physic, must
All follow this, and come to dust.

Fear no more the lightning-flash,
  Nor the all-dreaded thunder-stone,
Fear not slander, censure rash;
  Thou hast finished joy and moan:
All lovers young, all lovers must
Consign to thee, and come to dust.

No exorciser harm thee!
Nor no witchcraft charm thee!

Ghost unlaid forbear thee!
Nothing ill come near thee!
Quiet consummation have;
And renownèd be thy grave!
William Shakespeare.

"COME AWAY, COME AWAY, DEATH"

Come away, come away, death,
   And in sad cypress let me be laid;
Fly away, fly away, breath,
   I am slain by a fair cruel maid.
My shroud of white, stuck all with yew,
   O, prepare it!
My part of death, no one so true
   Did share it.

Not a flower, not a flower sweet,
   On my black coffin let there be strown;
Not a friend, not a friend greet
   My poor corpse, where my bones shall be thrown:
A thousand thousand sighs to save,
   Lay me, O, where
Sad true lover never find my grave,
   To weep there!   *William Shakespeare.*

SONG FOR SAINT CECILIA'S DAY

An ode on the power of music; Saint Cecilia was the legendary inventor of the organ.

From harmony, from heavenly harmony
   This universal frame began;
When Nature underneath a heap
   Of jarring atoms lay,

Song for Saint Cecilia's Day

And could not heave her head,
The tuneful voice was heard on high,
"Arise, ye more than dead!"
Then cold, and hot, and moist, and dry,
In order to their stations leap,
And Music's power obey.
From harmony, from heavenly harmony
  This universal frame began:
  From harmony to harmony
Through all the compass of the notes it ran,
The diapason[1] closing full in man.

What passion cannot Music raise and quell?
When Jubal[2] struck the chorded shell,
  His listening brethren stood around,
And, wondering, on their faces fell
  To worship that celestial sound:
Less than a god they thought there could not
    dwell
Within the hollow of that shell
That spoke so sweetly and so well.
What passion cannot Music raise and quell?

The trumpet's loud clangor
  Excites us to arms,
With shrill notes of anger
  And mortal alarms.
The double double double beat
  Of the thundering drum
Cries, "Hark! the foes come;
Charge! Charge! 'tis too late to retreat."

[1] The climax of the whole melody.
[2] In Genesis iv. 21 Jubal is named as "the father of all such as handle the harp and organ."

The soft complaining flute
  In dying notes discovers
  The woes of hopeless lovers,
Whose dirge is whispered by the warbling flute.

  Sharp violins proclaim
Their jealous pangs and desperation,
Fury, frantic indignation,
Depth of pains, and height of passion
  For the fair, disdainful dame.

But oh, what art can teach,
What human voice can reach
  The sacred organ's praise?
Notes inspiring holy love,
  Notes that wing their heavenly ways
To mend the choirs above.

Orpheus could lead the savage race
And trees uprooted left their place,
  Sequacious of the lyre;
But bright Cecilia raised the wonder higher:
  When to her organ vocal breath was given,
An angel heard, and straight appeared,
  Mistaking earth for heaven.

As from the power of sacred lays
  The spheres began to move,
And sung the great Creator's praise
  To all the blest above;
So when the last and dreadful hour
This crumbling pageant shall devour,
The trumpet shall be heard on high,
The dead shall live, the living die,
And Music shall untune the sky.

John Dryden.

BATTLE SONG

Ebenezer Elliott's "Battle Song" cannot be rightly understood unless the occasion which called it forth is known. Elliott was the poet of men who agitated for the repeal of the Corn Laws, which kept high the price of bread, and made life hard and difficult for the poor. This is a political poem, a trumpet-call to those who are oppressed. The resounding clang of its lines rings like the tramp of an army resolved to conquer or die, and marching to the destined field.

Day, like our souls, is fiercely dark;
    What then? 'Tis day!
We sleep no more; the cock crows—hark!
    To arms! away!
They come! they come! the knell is rung
    Of us or them;
Wide o'er their march the pomp is flung
    Of gold and gem.
What collared hound of lawless sway,
    To famine dear—
What pensioned slave of Attila,
    Leads in the rear?
Come they from Scythian wilds afar,
    Our blood to spill?
Wear they the livery of the Czar?
    They do his will.
Nor tasselled silk, nor epaulet,
    Nor plume, nor torse—
No splendour gilds, all sternly met,
    Our foot and horse;
But, dark and still, we inly glow,
    Condensed in ire!
Strike, tawdry slaves, and ye shall know
    Our gloom is fire.

In vain your pomp, ye evil powers,
    Insults the land;
Wrongs, vengeance, and the Cause are ours,
    And God's right hand!
Madmen! they trample into snakes
    The wormy clod!
Like fire, beneath their feet awakes
    The sword of God!
Behind, before, above, below,
    They rouse the brave;
Where'er they go, they make a foe,
    Or find a grave.

Ebenezer Elliott.

II
"IF ALL THE PENS THAT EVER POETS HELD"

If all the pens that ever poets held
Had fed the feeling of their masters' thoughts,
And every sweetness that inspired their hearts,
Their minds, and muses, on admirèd themes:—
If all the heavenly quintessence they still [1]
From their immortal flowers of poesy,
Wherein, as in a mirror, we perceive
The highest reaches of a human wit:—
If these had made one poem's period,
And all combined in beauty's worthiness,
Yet should there hover in their restless heads
One thought, one grace, one wonder, at the least,
Which into words no virtue can digest.

From "Tamburlaine," by Christopher Marlowe.

ODE

By some word-sorcery the author of this song has produced a poem which is like a charm, strange, unearthly, and sweet. He was a singer, and nothing more; the words have a rare beauty which is astonishing, but their meaning is simple. The poem on page 131, the "Chorus from Atalanta," is of the same kind.

We are the music makers,
  And we are the dreamers of dreams
Wandering by lone sea-breakers,
  And sitting by desolate streams:—
World-losers and world-forsakers,
  On whom the pale moon gleams:
Yet we are the movers and shakers
  Of the world for ever, it seems.

[1] Distil.

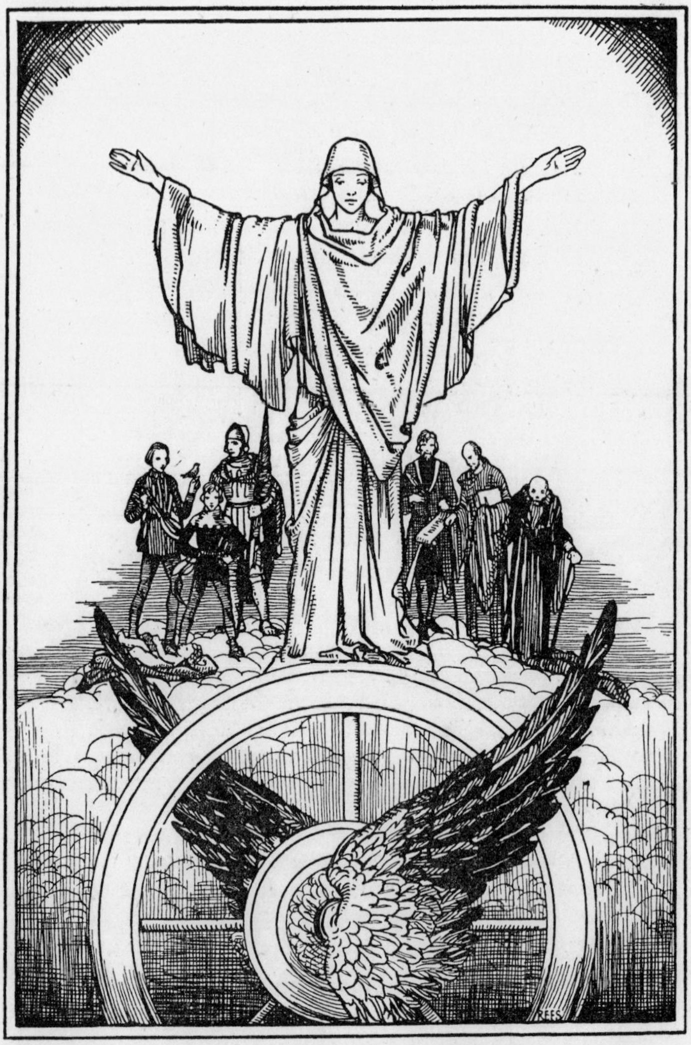

Ode

With wonderful deathless ditties
We build up the world's great cities,
　And out of a fabulous story
　We fashion an empire's glory:
One man with a dream, at pleasure,
　Shall go forth and conquer a crown;
And three with a new song's measure
　Can trample a kingdom down.

We, in the ages lying
　In the buried past of the earth,
Built Nineveh with our sighing,
　And Babel itself with our mirth;
And o'erthrew them with prophesying
　To the old of the new world's worth;
For each age is a dream that is dying,
　Or one that is coming to birth.
　　　　　　　Arthur O'Shaughnessy.

ON FIRST LOOKING INTO CHAPMAN'S HOMER

Scattered throughout this book will be found a number of sonnets. A sonnet is a poem of fourteen lines, and according to the way in which they are constructed sonnets may be classified. It might seem that so narrow a space as fourteen lines would cramp a poet, but it has been found to have the advantage of bringing out in sharp outline the nature of his thought, if he succeeds in expressing it adequately.

The sonnet was introduced from Italian in the sixteenth century. Many great poets have written sonnets, notably Shakespeare, Milton, and Wordsworth.

Much have I travelled in the realms of gold,
And many goodly states and kingdoms seen;
Round many western islands have I been
Which bards in fealty to Apollo hold.

Oft of one wide expanse had I been told
That deep-browed Homer ruled as his demesne:
Yet did I never breathe its pure serene
Till I heard Chapman speak out loud and bold:
Then felt I like some watcher of the skies
When a new planet swims into his ken;
Or like stout Cortez, when with eagle eyes
He stared at the Pacific, and all his men
Looked at each other with a wild surmise,
Silent, upon a peak in Darien.

John Keats.

LYCIDAS

"Lycidas" is a lament for the untimely death of the poet's friend, Edward King, who was drowned on a voyage to Ireland. It is cast in the form of a pastoral elegy, Milton and his friend being represented as shepherds. It contains a number of superb passages, and the whole piece reaches a point of excellence at which the voice of criticism is dumb.

YET once more, O ye Laurels, and once more,
Ye Myrtles brown, with Ivy never sere,
I come to pluck your berries harsh and crude,
And with forced fingers rude
Shatter your leaves before the mellowing year.
Bitter constraint, and sad occasion dear,
Compels me to disturb your season due:
For Lycidas is dead, dead ere his prime
Young Lycidas, and hath not left his peer:
Who would not sing for Lycidas? he knew
Himself to sing, and build the lofty rhyme.
He must not float upon his watery bier
Unwept, and welter to the parching wind
Without the meed of some melodious tear.

Lycidas

   Begin, then, Sisters of the sacred well,
That from the seat of Jove doth spring,
Begin, and somewhat loudly sweep the string.
Hence with denial vain and coy excuse;
So may some gentle Muse
With lucky words favour my destined urn,
And as he passes turn,
And bid fair peace be to my sable shroud.
   For we were nursed upon the self-same hill,
Fed the same flock, by fountain, shade, and rill.
Together both, ere the high lawns appeared
Under the opening eyelids of the morn,
We drove afield, and both together heard
What time the grey-fly winds her sultry horn,
Battening our flocks with the fresh dews of night,
Oft till the star that rose at evening bright
Towards heaven's descent had sloped his westering
   wheel.
Meanwhile the rural ditties were not mute,
Tempered to the oaten flute;
Rough satyrs danced, and fauns with cloven heel
From the glad sound would not be absent long,
And old Damœtas loved to hear our song.
   But O the heavy change, now thou art gone,
Now thou art gone, and never must return!
Thee, Shepherd, thee the woods and desert caves,
With wild thyme and the gadding vine o'ergrown,
And all their echoes, mourn.
The willows and the hazel copses green
Shall now no more be seen
Fanning their joyous leaves to thy soft lays.
As killing as the canker to the rose,
Or taint-worm to the weanling herds that graze,
Or frost to flowers that their gay wardrobe wear

When first the whitethorn blows,
Such, Lycidas, thy loss to Shepherd's ear.
  Where were ye, nymphs, when the remorseless deep
Closed o'er the head of your loved Lycidas?
For neither were ye playing on the steep
Where your old bards, the famous druids, lie,
Nor on the shaggy top of Mona [1] high,
Nor yet where Deva [2] spreads her wizard stream.
Ay me, I fondly dream
"Had ye been there"—for what could that have done?
What could the Muse herself that Orpheus bore,
The Muse herself, for her enchanting son,
Whom universal nature did lament,
When by the rout that made the hideous roar,
His gory visage down the stream was sent,
Down the swift Hebrus to the Lesbian shore?
  Alas! what boots it with incessant care
To tend the homely, slighted, shepherd's trade,
And strictly meditate the thankless Muse?
Were it not better done, as others use,
To sport with Amaryllis in the shade,
Or with the tangles of Neæra's hair?
Fame is the spur that the clear spirit doth raise
(That last infirmity of noble minds)
To scorn delights and live laborious days:
But the fair guerdon when we hope to find,
And think to burst out into sudden blaze,
Comes the blind Fury with the abhorrèd shears,
And slits the thin-spun life. "But not the praise,"
Phœbus replied, and touched my trembling ears;

[1] The isle of Anglesey.   [2] The River Dee

Lycidas

"Fame is no plant that grows on mortal soil,
Nor in the glistering foil
Set off to the world, nor in broad rumour lies,
But lives and spreads aloft by those pure eyes,
And perfect witness of all-judging Jove;
As he pronounces lastly on each deed,
Of so much fame in Heaven expect thy meed."
　O fountain Arethuse, and thou honoured flood,
Smooth-sliding Mincius, crowned with vocal reeds!
That strain I heard was of a higher mood:
But now my oat proceeds,
And listens to the Herald of the Sea,
That came in Neptune's plea.
He asked the waves, and asked the felon winds,
"What hard mishap hath doomed this gentle swain?"
And questioned every gust of rugged wings
That blows from off each beaked promontory:
They knew not of his story;
And sage Hippotades[1] their answer brings,
That not a blast was from his dungeon strayed:
The air was calm, and on the level brine
Sleek Panope[2] with all her sisters played.
It was that fatal and perfidious bark,
Built in the eclipse, and rigged with curses dark,
That sunk so low that sacred head of thine.
　Next Camus,[3] reverend sire, went footing slow,
His mantle hairy, and his bonnet sedge,
Inwrought with figures dim, and on the edge
Like to that sanguine flower inscribed with woe.

[1] The god of the winds.　　[2] A sea-nymph.
[3] The River Cam.

"Ah, who hath reft," quoth he, "my dearest pledge?"
Last came, and last did go,
The Pilot of the Galilean lake;[1]
Two massy keys he bore, of metals twain
(The golden opes, the iron shuts amain);
He shook his mitred locks, and stern bespake:
"How well could I have spared for thee, young swain,
Enow of such as, for their bellies' sake,
Creep, and intrude, and climb into the fold!
Of other care they little reckoning make
Than how to scramble at the shearers' feast,
And shove away the worthy bidden guest.
Blind mouths! that scarce themselves know how to hold
A sheep-hook, or have learnt aught else the least
That to the faithful herdman's art belongs!
What recks it them? What need they?—They are sped.
And, when they list, their lean and flashy songs
Grate on their scrannel pipes of wretched straw.
The hungry sheep look up, and are not fed,
But, swollen with wind and the rank mist they draw,
Rot inwardly, and foul contagion spread;
Besides what the grim wolf, with privy paw,
Daily devours apace, and nothing said:
But that two-handed engine at the door
Stands ready to smite once, and smite no more."
 Return, Alpheus, the dread voice is past
That shrunk thy streams; return, Sicilian Muse,

[1] St. Peter.

And call the vales, and bid them hither cast
Their bells and flowerets of a thousand hues.
Ye valleys low, where the mild whispers use
Of shades, and wanton winds, and gushing brooks,
On whose fresh lap the swart star sparely looks,
Throw hither all your quaint enamelled eyes,
That on the green turf suck the honeyed showers,
And purple all the ground with vernal flowers;
Bring the rathe [1] primrose that forsaken dies,
The tufted crow-toe, and pale jessamine,
The white pink, and the pansy freaked with jet,
The glowing violet,
The musk-rose, and the well-attired woodbine,
With cowslips wan, that hang the pensive head,
And every flower that sad embroidery wears;
Bid amaranthus all his beauty shed,
And daffodillies fill their cups with tears,
To strew the laureate hearse where Lycid lies.
For, so to interpose a little ease,
Let our frail thoughts dally with false surmise—
Ay me!—whilst thee the shores and sounding seas
Wash far away, where'er thy bones are hurled,
Whether beyond the stormy Hebrides,
Where thou, perhaps, under the whelming tide
Visit'st the bottom of the monstrous world,
Or whether thou, to our moist vows denied,
Sleep'st by the fable of Bellerus old,
Where the great vision of the guarded mount [2]
Looks toward Namancos and Bayona's hold.
Look homeward, Angel, now, and melt with ruth;
And, O ye Dolphins, waft the hapless youth.

[1] Early.
[2] St. Michael's Mount. Bellerus was a Cornish giant.

Weep no more, woful shepherds, weep no more ;
For Lycidas, your sorrow, is not dead,
Sunk though he be beneath the watery floor ;
So sinks the day-star in the ocean bed,
And yet anon repairs his drooping head,
And tricks his beams, and with new-spangled ore
Flames in the forehead of the morning sky.
So Lycidas sunk low, but mounted high
Through the dear might of Him that walked the waves,
Where, other groves and other streams along,
With nectar pure his oozy locks he laves,
And hears the unexpressive nuptial song,
In the blest kingdoms meek of joy and love.
There entertain him all the saints above,
In solemn troops, and sweet societies,
That sing, and singing in their glory move,
And wipe the tears for ever from his eyes.
Now, Lycidas, the shepherds weep no more ;
Henceforth thou art the Genius of the Shore,
In thy large recompense, and shalt be good
To all that wander in that perilous flood.

Thus sang the uncouth swain to the oaks and rills,
While the still morn went out with sandals grey.
He touched the tender stops of various quills,
With eager thought warbling his Doric lay.
And now the sun had stretched out all the hills,
And now was dropped into the western bay.
At last he rose, and twitched his mantle blue ;
To-morrow to fresh woods, and pastures new.

John Milton.

IN MEMORIAM A. H.

A. H. was Auberon Herbert, Lord Lucas, Captain in the Royal Flying Corps, killed in France on November 3, 1916. This poem may be regarded as an elegy upon all the airmen who lost their lives during the Great War.

The wind had blown away the rain
That all day long had soaked the level plain.
Against the horizon's fiery wrack
The sheds loomed black.
And higher, in their tumultuous concourse met,
The streaming clouds, shot-riddled banners, wet
With the flickering storm,
Drifted and smouldered, warm
With flashes sent
From the lower firmament.
And they concealed—
They only here and there through rifts revealed
A hidden sanctuary of fire and light,
A city of chrysolite.

We looked and laughed and wondered, and I said
That orange sea, those oriflammes outspread,
Were like the fanciful imaginings
That the young painter flings
Upon the canvas bold,
Such as the sage and the old
Make mock at, saying it could never be;
And you assented also, laughingly.
I wondered what they meant,
That flaming firmament,
Those clouds so grey so gold, so wet so warm,
So much of glory and so much of storm,
The end of the world, or the end
Of the war—remoter still to me and you, my friend.

Alas, it meant not this, it meant not that:
It meant that now the last time you and I
Should look at the golden sky,
And the dark fields large and flat,
And smell the evening weather,
And laugh and talk and wonder both together.

The last, last time. We nevermore should meet
In France or London street,
Or fields of home. The desolated space
Of life shall nevermore
Be what it was before.
No one shall take your place.
No other face
Can fill that empty frame.
There is no answer when we call your name.
We cannot hear your step upon the stair.
We turn to speak and find a vacant chair.
Something is broken which we cannot mend.
God has done more than take away a friend
In taking you; for all that we have left
Is bruised and irremediably bereft.
There is none like you. Yet not that alone
Do we bemoan;
But this; that you were greater than the rest,
And better than the best.

O liberal heart fast-rooted to the soil,
O lover of ancient freedom and proud toil,
Friend of the gipsies and all wandering song,
The forest's nursling and the favoured child
Of woodlands wild—
O brother to the birds and all things free,
Captain of liberty!

In Memoriam A. H.

Deep in your heart the restless seed was sown;
The vagrant spirit fretted in your feet;
We wondered could you tarry long,
And brook for long the cramping street,
Or would you one day sail for shores unknown,
And shake from you the dust of towns, and spurn
The crowded market-place—and not return?
You found a sterner guide;
You heard the guns. Then, to their distant fire,
Your dreams were laid aside;
And, on that day, you cast your heart's desire
Upon a burning pyre;
You gave your service to the exalted need,
Until at last from bondage freed,
At liberty to serve as you loved best,
You chose the noblest way. God did the rest.

So, when the spring of the world shall shrive our stain,
After the winter of war,
When the poor world awakes to peace once more,
After such night of ravage and of rain,
You shall not come again.
You shall not come to taste the old spring weather,
To gallop through the soft untrampled heather,
To bathe and bake your body on the grass.
We shall be there; alas,
But not with you! When spring shall wake the earth,
And quicken the scarred fields to the new birth,
Our grief shall grow. For what can spring renew
More fiercely for us than the need of you?

That night I dreamt they sent for me and said
That you were missing, "missing, missing—
    dead":
I cried when in the morning I awoke,
And all the world seemed shrouded in a cloak;
But when I saw the sun,
And knew another day had just begun,
I brushed the dream away, and quite forgot
The nightmare's ugly blot.
So was the dream forgot. The dream came true.
Before the night I knew
That you had flown away into the air
For ever. Then I cheated my despair.
I said
That you were safe—or wounded—but not dead.
Alas! I knew
Which was the false and true.

And after days of watching, days of lead,
There came the certain news that you were dead.
You had died fighting, fighting against odds,
Such as in war the gods
Ætherial dared when all the world was young;
Such fighting as blind Homer never sung,
Nor Hector nor Achilles never knew,
High in the empty blue.

High, high, above the clouds, against the setting
    sun,
The fight was fought, and your great task was
    done.

Of all your brave adventures this the last
The bravest was and best;

In Memoriam A. H.

Meet ending to a long embattled past,
This swift, triumphant, fatal quest,
Crowned with the wreath that never perisheth,
And diadem of honourable death;
Swift Death aflame with offering supreme
And mighty sacrifice,
More than all mortal dream;
A soaring death, and near to Heaven's gate;
Beneath the very walls of Paradise.
Surely with soul elate,
You heard the destined bullet as you flew,
And surely your prophetic spirit knew
That you had well deserved that shining fate.

Here is no waste,
No burning might-have-been,
No bitter after-taste,
None to censure, none to screen,
Nothing awry, nor anything misspent;
Only content, content beyond content,
Which hath not any room for betterment.

God, who made you valiant, strong, and swift,
And maimed you with a bullet long ago,
And cleft your riotous ardour with a rift,
And checked your youth's tumultuous overflow,
Gave back your youth to you,
And packed in moments rare and few
Achievements manifold
And happiness untold,
And bade you spring to Death as to a bride,
In manhood's ripeness, power, and pride,
And on your sandals the strong wings of youth.

He let you leave a name
To shine on the entablatures of truth,
For ever;
To sound for ever in answering halls of fame.

For you soared onward to the world which rags
Of clouds, like tattered flags,
Concealed; you reached the walls of chrysolite,
The mansions white;
And losing all, you gained the civic crown
Of that eternal town,
Wherein you passed a rightful citizen
Of the bright commonwealth ablaze beyond our
    ken.

Surely you found companions meet for you
In that high place;
You met there face to face
Those you had never known, but whom you
    knew;
Knights of the Table Round,
And all the very brave, the very true,
With chivalry crowned;
The captains rare,
Courteous and brave beyond our human air;
Those who had loved and suffered overmuch,
Now free from the world's touch.
And with them were the friends of yesterday,
Who went before and pointed you the way;
And in that place of freshness, light, and rest,
Where Lancelot and Tristram vigil keep
Over their King's long sleep,

In Memoriam A. H.

Surely they made a place for you,
Their long-expected guest,
Among the chosen few,
And welcomed you, their brother and their friend,
To that companionship which hath no end.

And in the portals of the sacred hall
You hear the trumpet's call,
At dawn upon the silvery battlement,
Re-echo through the deep,
And bid the sons of God to rise from sleep,
And with a shout to hail
The sunrise on the city of the Grail;
The music that proud Lucifer in Hell
Missed more than all the joys that he forwent.
You hear the solemn bell
At vesper, when the oriflammes are furled;
And then you know that somewhere in the world,
That shines far-off beneath you like a gem,
They think of you, and when you think of them
You know that they will wipe away their tears,
And cast aside their fears;
That they will have it so,
And in no other wise;
That it is well with them because they know,
With faithful eyes,
Fixed forward and turned upwards to the skies,
That it is well with you,
Among the chosen few,
Among the very brave, the very true.

Maurice Baring.

ON THE COUNTESS DOWAGER OF PEMBROKE

Underneath this sable hearse
Lies the subject of all verse:
Sidney's sister, Pembroke's mother:
Death, ere thou hast slain another
Fair and learn'd and good as she,
Time shall throw a dart at thee.

William Browne.

IL PENSEROSO

"Il Penseroso" is a companion poem to "L'Allegro," being a kind of verse-essay or song upon the mood of serious contemplation. Melancholy does not mean in it sadness so much as sobermindedness, things and events being described as they appear to the reflective mind. Delightful rhythm and graceful fancy meet in it, and the tone of its exquisitely modulated eight-syllabled couplet verse never jars upon the reader's ear.

Hence, vain deluding joys,
  The brood of Folly, without father bred!
How little you bestead,
  Or fill the fixèd mind with all your toys!
Dwell in some idle brain,
  And fancies fond with gaudy shapes possess,
As thick and numberless
  As the gay motes that people the sunbeams,
Or likest hovering dreams,
  The fickle pensioners of Morpheus' train.
But hail, thou goddess sage and holy!
Hail, divinest Melancholy!
Whose saintly visage is too bright
To hit the sense of human sight;

Il Penseroso 33

And therefore to our weaker view
O'erlaid with black, staid Wisdom's hue;
Black, but such as in esteem
Prince Memnon's sister might beseem,
Or that starred Ethiop queen that strove
To set her beauty's praise above
The sea-nymphs, and their powers offended.
Yet thou art higher far descended:
Thee, bright-haired Vesta, long of yore
To solitary Saturn bore;
His daughter she: in Saturn's reign
Such mixture was not held a stain.
Oft in glimmering bowers and glades
He met her, and in secret shades
Of woody Ida's inmost grove,
Whilst yet there was no fear of Jove.
   Come, pensive nun, devout and pure,
Sober, steadfast, and demure,
All in a robe of darkest grain,
Flowing with majestic train,
And sable stole of cypress lawn
Over thy decent shoulders drawn.
Come, but keep thy wonted state,
With even step, and musing gait,
And looks commercing with the skies,
Thy rapt soul sitting in thine eyes:
There, held in holy passion still,
Forget thyself to marble, till,
With a sad leaden downward cast,
Thou fix them on the earth as fast.
And join with thee calm Peace and Quiet,
Spare Fast, that oft with gods doth diet,
And hears the Muses in a ring,
Aye round about Jove's altar sing:

And add to these retirèd Leisure,
That in trim gardens takes his pleasure;
But, first and chiefest, with thee bring
Him that yon soars on golden wing,
Guiding the fiery-wheelèd throne,
The cherub Contemplation;
And the mute Silence hist along,
'Less Philomel will deign a song,
In her sweetest saddest plight,
Smoothing the rugged brow of Night,
While Cynthia checks her dragon yoke
Gently o'er the accustomed oak.
Sweet bird, that shunn'st the noise of folly,
Most musical, most melancholy!
Thee, chauntress, oft the woods among
I woo, to hear thy even-song;
And, missing thee, I walk unseen
On the dry smooth-shaven green,
To behold the wandering moon,
Riding near her highest noon,
Like one that had been led astray
Through the heaven's wide pathless way;
And oft, as if her head she bowed,
Stooping through a fleecy cloud,
    Oft, on a plat of rising ground,
I hear the far-off curfew sound,
Over some wide-watered shore,
Swinging slow with sullen roar;
Or if the air will not permit,
Some still removèd place will fit,
Where glowing embers through the room
Teach light to counterfeit a gloom,
Far from all resort of mirth
Save the cricket on the hearth,

Or the bellman's drowsy charm
To bless the doors from nightly harm.
Or let my lamp, at midnight hour,
Be seen in some high lonely tower,
Where I may oft outwatch the Bear,
With thrice-great Hermes, or unsphere
The spirit of Plato, to unfold
What worlds or what vast regions hold
The immortal mind that hath forsook
Her mansion in this fleshly nook;
And of those demons that are found
In fire, air, flood, or underground,
Whose power hath a true consent
With planet or with element.
Sometime let gorgeous tragedy
In sceptred pall come sweeping by,
Presenting Thebes, or Pelops' line,
Or the tale of Troy divine,
Or what, though rare, of later age
Ennobled hath the buskined stage.

But, O sad Virgin! that thy power
Might raise Musæus from his bower;
Or bid the soul of Orpheus sing
Such notes as, warbled to the string,
Drew iron tears down Pluto's cheek,
And made Hell grant what love did seek.
Or call up him that left half-told
The story of Cambuscan bold,
Of Camball, and of Algarsife,
And who had Canace to wife,
That owned the virtuous ring and glass,
And of the wondrous horse of brass
On which the Tartar king did ride;
And if aught else great bards beside

In sage and solemn tunes have sung,
Of tourneys and of trophies hung,
Of forests and enchantments drear,
Where more is meant than meets the ear.
   Thus, Night, oft see me in thy pale career,
Till civil-suited Morn appear,
Not tricked and frounced, as she was wont
With the Attic boy to hunt,
But kerchieft in a comely cloud,
While rocking winds are piping loud,
Or ushered with a shower still,
When the gust hath blown his fill,
Ending on the rustling leaves,
With minute drops from off the eaves.
And, when the sun begins to fling
His glaring beams, me, Goddess, bring
To archèd walks of twilight groves,
And shadows brown that Sylvan loves,
Of pine, or monumental oak,
Where the rude axe with heavèd stroke
Was never heard the nymphs to daunt,
Or fright them from their hallowed haunt.
There, in close covert, by some brook,
Where no profaner eye may look,
Hide me from day's garish eye,
While the bee with honeyed thigh,
That at her flowery work doth sing,
And the waters murmuring
With such consort as they keep,
Entice the dewy-feathered sleep.
And let some strange mysterious dream
Wave at his wings, in airy stream
Of lively portraiture displayed,
Softly in my eyelids laid ;

Il Penseroso

And, as I wake, sweet music breathe
Above, about, or underneath,
Sent by some spirit to mortals good,
Or the unseen genius of the wood.
　But let my due feet never fail
To walk the studious cloister's pale,
And love the high embowèd roof,
With antique pillars massy-proof,
And storied windows richly dight,
Casting a dim religious light.
There let the pealing organ blow,
To the full-voiced choir below,
In service high and anthems clear,
As may with sweetness, through mine ear,
Dissolve me into ecstasies,
And bring all Heaven before mine eyes.
And may at last my weary age
Find out the peaceful hermitage,
The hairy gown and mossy cell,
Where I may sit and rightly spell
Of every star that heaven doth show,
And every herb that sips the dew;
Till old experience do attain
To something like prophetic strain.
　These pleasures, Melancholy, give,
And I with thee will choose to live.

John Milton.

LYING IN THE GRASS

Between two russet tufts of summer grass
I watch the world through hot air as through glass,
And by my face sweet lights and colours pass.

Before me, dark against the fading sky,
I watch three mowers mowing, as I lie :
With brawny arms they sweep in harmony.

Brown English faces by the sun burnt red,
Rich glowing colour on bare throat and head,
My heart would leap to watch them, were I
    dead !

And in my strong young living as I lie,
I seem to move with them in harmony,—
A fourth is mowing, and that fourth am I.

The music of the scythes that glide and leap,
The young men whistling as their great arms
    sweep,
And all the perfume and sweet sense of sleep,

The weary butterflies that droop their wings,
The dreamy nightingale that hardly sings,
And all the lassitude of happy things,

Is mingling with the warm and pulsing blood
That gushes through my veins a languid flood,
And feeds my spirit as the sap a bud.

Behind the mowers, on the amber air,
A dark-green beech-wood rises, still and fair,
A white path winding up it like a stair.

And see that girl, with pitcher on her head,
And clean white apron on her gown of red,—
Her even-song of love is but half-said :

Lying in the Grass

She waits the youngest mower.   Now he goes;
Her cheeks are redder than the wild blush-rose;
They climb up where the deepest shadows close.

Ah! now the rosy children come to play,
And romp and struggle with the new-mown hay;
Their clear high voices sound from far away.

They know so little why the world is sad,
They dig themselves warm graves and yet are
    glad;
Their muffled screams and laughter make me
    mad!

I long to go and play among them there,
Unseen, like wind, to take them by the hair,
And gently make their rosy cheeks more fair.

The happy children, full of frank surprise,
And sudden whims and innocent ecstasies;
What godhead sparkles from their liquid eyes!

No wonder round those urns of mingled clays
That Tuscan potters fashioned in old days,
And coloured like the torrid earth ablaze,

We find the little gods and loves portrayed
Through ancient forests wandering undismayed,
Or gathered, whispering, in some pleasant glade.

They knew, as I do now, what keen delight
A strong man feels to watch the tender flight
Of little children playing in his sight.

I do not hunger for a well-stored mind,
I only wish to live my life, and find
My heart in unison with all mankind.

My life is like the single dewy star
That trembles on the horizon's primrose-bar,—
A microcosm where all things living are.

And if, among the noiseless grasses, Death
Should come behind and take away my breath,
I should not rise as one who sorroweth;

For I should pass, but all the world would be
Full of desire and young delight and glee,
And why should men be sad through loss of me?

The light is dying; in the silver-blue
The young moon shines from her bright window
    through;
The mowers all are gone, and I go too.
Sir Edmund Gosse.

WORLDLY PARADISE

Who can live in heart so glad
As the merry country lad?
Who upon a fair green balk
May at pleasure sit and walk,
And amid the azure skies
See the morning sun arise;
While he hears in every spring
How the birds do chirp and sing;
Or, before the hounds in cry,
See the hare go stealing by:

Worldly Paradise

> Or, along the shallow brook,
> Angling with a baited hook,
> See the fishes leap and play
> In a blessed sunny day:
> Or to hear the partridge call,
> Till she have her covey all:
> Or to see the subtle fox,
> How the villain plies the box;
> After feeding on his prey
> How he closely sneaks away.
> Through the hedge and down the furrow
> Till he gets into his burrow:
> Then the bee to gather honey,
> And the little black-haired coney,
> On a bank for sunny place
> With her forefeet wash her face:
> Are not these, with thousands moe
> Than the courts of kings do know,
> The true pleasing spirit's sights,
> That may breed true love's delights?
>
> *Nicholas Breton.*

THE SOLDIER

If I should die, think only this of me:
  That there's some corner of a foreign field
That is for ever England. There shall be
  In that rich earth a richer dust concealed;
A dust whom England bore, shaped, made aware,
  Gave, once, her flowers to love, her ways to roam,
A body of England's, breathing English air,
  Washed by the rivers, blest by suns of home.

And think, this heart, all evil shed away,
    A pulse in the eternal mind, no less
Gives somewhere back the thoughts by England
    given;
    Her sights and sounds; dreams happy as her
        day;
And laughter, learnt of friends; and gentleness,
    In hearts at peace, under an English heaven.
Rupert Brooke.

THE VOLUNTEER

"He leapt to arms unbidden,
    Unneeded, overbold;
His face by earth is hidden,
    His heart in earth is cold.

"Curse on the reckless daring
    That could not wait the call,
The proud fantastic bearing
    That would be first to fall!"

O tears of human passion,
    Blur not the image true;
This was not folly's fashion,
    This was the man we knew.
Henry Newbolt.

BRUMANA

No better expression of the feeling of homesickness has ever been written than these lines from Syria, where the poet thought of the landscape, and especially of the pine-trees, of England. In the next poem another and less passionate poet tells, in words equally beautiful, of wanderers who lost the longing for home. This latter poem was suggested by some lines of Homer

Brumana

about the arrival in Egypt of Odysseus and his mariners. In both poems a prominent feature is the lovely scenery that is described.

Oh, shall I never, never be home again?
Meadows of England shining in the rain,
Spread wide your daisied lawns; your ramparts green
With briar fortify; with blossom screen
Till my far morning; and, O streams that slow,
And pure, and deep, through plains and playlands go,
For me your love and all your kingcups store;
And, dark militia of the southern shore,
Old fragrant friends, preserve me the last lines
Of that long saga which you sang me, pines,
When, lonely boy, beneath the chosen tree
I listened, with my eyes upon the sea.

O traitor pines, you sang what life has found
The falsest of fair tales.
Earth blew a far-horn prelude all around,
That native music of her forest home,
While, from the sea's blue fields and syren dales,
Shadows and light noon-spectres of the foam,
Riding the summer gales,
On aery viols plucked an idle sound.

Hearing you sing, O trees,
Hearing you murmur, "There are older seas,
That beat on vaster sands,
Where the wise snailfish move their pearly towers
To carven rocks and sculptured promont'ries."
Hearing you whisper, "Lands
Where blaze the unimaginable flowers."

Beneath me in the valley waves the palm,
Beneath, beyond the valley, breaks the sea ;
Beneath me sleep in mist and light and calm
Cities of Lebanon, dream-shadow-dim,
Where kings of Tyre and kings of Tyre did rule
In ancient days in endless dynasty ;
And all around the snowy mountains swim
Like mighty swans afloat in heaven's pool.

But I will walk upon the wooded hill
Where stands a grove, O pines, of sister pines,
And when the downy twilight droops her wing
And no sea glimmers and no mountain shines
My heart shall listen still.
For pines are gossip pines the wide world through
And full of runic tales to sigh or sing.
'Tis ever sweet through pines to see the sky
Mantling a deeper gold or darker blue.
'Tis ever sweet to lie
On the dry carpet of the needles brown,
And though the fanciful green lizard stir
And windy odours light as thistledown
Breathe from the lavdanon and lavender,
Half to forget the wandering and pain,
Half to remember days that have gone by,
And dream and dream that I am home again.

James Elroy Flecker.

THE LOTOS-EATERS

"COURAGE!" he said, and pointed toward the land,
"This mounting wave will roll us shoreward soon."
In the afternoon they came unto a land
In which it seemèd always afternoon.

The Lotos-eaters

All round the coast the languid air did swoon,
Breathing like one that hath a weary dream.
Full-faced above the valley stood the moon;
And, like a downward smoke, the slender stream
Along the cliff to fall and pause and fall did seem.

A land of streams! some, like a downward smoke,
Slow-dropping veils of thinnest lawn, did go;
And some thro' wavering lights and shadows broke,
Rolling a slumbrous sheet of foam below.
They saw the gleaming river seaward flow
From the inner land: far off, three mountain-tops,
Three silent pinnacles of aged snow,
Stood sunset-flushed: and, dewed with showery drops,
Upclomb the shadowy pine above the woven copse.

The charmèd sunset lingered low adown
In the red west: thro' mountain clefts the dale
Was seen far inland, and the yellow down
Bordered with palm, and many a winding vale
And meadow, set with slender galingale;
A land where all things always seemed the same!
And round about the keel with faces pale,
Dark faces pale against that rosy flame,
The mild-eyed melancholy Lotos-eaters came.

Branches they bore of that enchanted stem,
Laden with flower and fruit, whereof they gave
To each, but whoso did receive of them,
And taste, to him the gushing of the wave
Far, far away did seem to mourn and rave

On alien shores; and if his fellow spake,
His voice was thin, as voices from the grave;
And deep-asleep he seemed, yet all awake,
And music in his ears his beating heart did make.

They sat them down upon the yellow sand,
Between the sun and moon upon the shore;
And sweet it was to dream of Fatherland,
Of child, and wife, and slave; but evermore
Most weary seemed the sea, weary the oar,
Weary the wandering fields of barren foam.
Then some one said: "We will return no more";
And all at once they sang: "Our island home
Is far beyond the wave; we will no longer roam."

Lord Tennyson.

SONNET

There was an Indian, who had known no change,
Who strayed content along a sunlit beach
Gathering shells. He heard a sudden strange
Commingled noise; looked up; and gasped for speech.
For in the bay, where nothing was before,
Moved on the sea, by magic, huge canoes,
With bellying cloths on poles, and not one oar,
And fluttering coloured signs and clambering crews.
And he, in fear, this naked man alone,
His fallen hands forgetting all their shells,
His lips gone pale, knelt low behind a stone,
And stared, and saw, and did not understand,
Columbus's doom-burdened caravels
Slant to the shore, and all their seamen land.

J. C. Squire.

"SOUND, SOUND THE CLARION!"

Sound, sound the clarion! Fill the fife!
    To all the sensual world proclaim
One crowded hour of glorious life
    Is worth an age without a name.

Sir Walter Scott.

INTO BATTLE

Captain the Hon. Julian Grenfell, D.S.O., 1st Royal Dragoons, who composed "Into Battle," was killed in action during the European War. He was a fighting man, and wrote scarcely any other poetry. Of this poem the late Sir Walter Raleigh said: "This is one of the great things in English literature. It is safe for ever; I know it by heart, and I never learned it. It has that queer property which only the best poems have, that a good many of the lines have more meaning than there is any need for."

The naked earth is warm with Spring,
    And with green grass and bursting trees
Leans to the sun's gaze glorying,
    And quivers in the sunny breeze;

And Life is Colour and Warmth and Light,
    And a striving evermore for these;
And he is dead who will not fight;
    And who dies fighting has increase.

The fighting man shall from the sun
    Take warmth, and life from the glowing earth;
Speed with the light-foot winds to run,
    And with the trees to newer birth;
And find, when fighting shall be done,
    Great rest, and fullness after dearth.

All the bright company of Heaven
  Hold him in their high comradeship,
The Dog-Star, and the Sisters Seven,
  Orion's belt and sworded hip.

The woodland trees that stand together,
  They stand to him each one a friend;
They gently speak in the windy weather;
  They guide to valley and ridges' end.

The kestrel hovering by day,
  And the little owls that call by night,
Bid him be swift and keen as they,
  As keen of ear, as swift of sight.

The blackbird sings to him, "Brother, brother,
  If this be the last song you shall sing,
Sing well, for you may not sing another;
  Brother, sing."

In dreary doubtful waiting hours,
  Before the brazen frenzy starts,
The horses show him nobler powers;
  O patient eyes, courageous hearts!

And when the burning moment breaks,
  And all things else are out of mind,
And only Joy-of-battle takes
  Him by the throat, and makes him blind,

Through joy and blindness he shall know,
  Not caring much to know, that still
Nor lead nor steel shall reach him, so
  That it be not the Destined Will.

Into Battle

The thundering line of battle stands,
    And in the air Death moans and sings;
But Day shall clasp him with strong hands,
    And Night shall fold him in soft wings.

Julian Grenfell.

FLANDERS, *April* 1915.

"CHILDE ROLAND TO THE DARK TOWER CAME"

"Childe Roland to the Dark Tower came" is a line quoted by Shakespeare from an old song on the romance of Childe Roland, who went on a quest to the rescue of his sister and brothers. This poem leaves its whole story to be worked out by the reader's imagination, merely presenting us with the adventurer's thoughts as he rides toward the place of trial. Sick apprehension fills his mind, the wonderful manner in which the poet describes the country through which he passes being the means by which it is revealed. The various scenes take on aspects belonging not so much to themselves as to his mood—the river is "spiteful," the cripple seems to be a secret and malignant foe, the sunset a "grim, red leer." Although objects become almost grotesque under the stress of his feelings, the art in the poem is true to life: everyone who has had to go on a disagreeable or dreadful errand will recognize the vivid and ghastly scenery which the poet creates with brief, decisive strokes.

My first thought was, he lied in every word,
That hoary cripple, with malicious eye
Askance to watch the working of his lie
On mine, and mouth scarce able to afford
Suppression of the glee that pursed and scored
Its edge, at one more victim gained thereby.

What else should he be set for, with his staff?
What, save to waylay with his lies, ensnare

All travellers who might find him posted there,
And ask the road? I guessed what skull-like
    laugh
Would break, what crutch 'gin write my epitaph
For pastime on the dusty thoroughfare.

So, quiet as despair, I turned from him,
That hateful cripple, out of his highway
Into the path he pointed. All the day
Had been a dreary one at best, and dim
Was settling to its close, yet shot one grim
Red leer to see the plain catch its estray.[1]

For mark! no sooner was I fairly found
Pledged to the plain, after a pace or two,
Than, pausing to throw backward a last view
O'er the safe road, 'twas gone! grey plain all
    around,
Nothing but plain to the horizon's bound.
I might go on: nought else remained to do.

So, on I went: I think I never saw
Such starved ignoble nature; nothing throve:
For flowers—as well expect a cedar grove!
But cockle, spurge, according to their law
Might propagate their kind, with none to awe,
You'd think: a burr had been a treasure-trove.

As for the grass, it grew as scant as hair
In leprosy: thin dry blades pricked the mud
Which underneath looked kneaded up with blood.
One stiff blind horse, his every bone a-stare,
Stood stupefied, however he came there,
Thrust out past service from the devil's stud.

[1] Fugitive.

"*Childe Roland to the Dark Tower came*" 51

A sudden little river crossed my path
As unexpected as a serpent comes.
No sluggish tide congenial to the glooms;
This, as it frothed by, might have been a bath
For the fiend's glowing hoof—to see the wrath
Of its black eddy bespate with flakes and spumes.

So petty, yet so spiteful! All along
Low scrubby alders kneeled down over it;
Drenched willows flung them headlong in a fit
Of mute despair, a suicidal throng:
The river which had done them all the wrong,
Whate'er that was, rolled by, deterred no whit.

Which, while I forded—good saints, how I feared
To set my foot upon a dead man's cheek,
Each step, or feel the spear I thrust to seek
For hollows, tangled in his hair or beard!—
It may have been a water-rat I speared,
But, ugh! it sounded like a baby's shriek.

And more than that—a furlong on—why, there!
What bad use was that engine for, that wheel,
Or brake, not wheel—that harrow fit to reel
Men's bodies out like silk? with all the air
Of Tophet's tool, on earth left unaware,
Or brought to sharpen its rusty teeth of steel.

Then came a bit of stubbed ground, once a wood,
Next a marsh, it would seem, and now mere earth
Desperate and done with; (so a fool finds mirth,
Makes a thing and then mars it, till his mood

52 A Book of English Poems

Changes and off he goes!) within a rood—
Bog, clay and rubble, sand and stark black dearth.

And just as far as ever from the end;
Nought in the distance but the evening, nought
To point my footstep further!—at the thought
A great black bird, Apollyon's bosom-friend,
Sailed past, nor beat his wide wing dragon-penned
That brushed my cap—perchance the guide I
    sought.

For, looking up, aware I somehow grew,
'Spite of the dusk, the plain had given place
All round to mountains—with such name to grace
Mere ugly heights and heaps now stolen in view.
How thus they had surprised me, solve it, you!
How to get from them was no clearer case.

Burningly it came on me all at once,
This was the place! those two hills on the right,
Crouched like two bulls locked horn in horn in
    fight;
While to the left, a tall scalped mountain . . .
    Dunce!
Dotard! a-dozing at the very nonce,
After a life spent training for the sight!

What in the midst lay but the Tower itself?
The round squat turret, blind as the fool's heart,
Built of brown stone, without a counterpart
In the whole world. The tempest's mocking elf
Points to the shipman thus the unseen shelf
He strikes on, only when the timbers start.

"*Child Roland to the Dark Tower came*" 53

Not see? because of night perhaps?—Why, day
Came back again for that! before it left,
The dying sunset kindled through a cleft:
The hills, like giants at a hunting, lay—
Chin upon hand, to see the game at bay,
"Now stab and end the creature—to the heft!"

Not hear? when noise was everywhere! It tolled
Increasing like a bell. Names in my ears
Of all the lost adventurers my peers,—
How such a one was strong, and such was bold,
And such was fortunate, yet each of old
Lost, lost! one moment knelled the woe of years.

There they stood, ranged along the hillsides, met
To view the last of me, a living frame
For one more picture! In a sheet of flame
I saw them and I knew them all. And yet
Dauntless the slug-horn to my lips I set,
And blew. "*Childe Roland to the Dark Tower came.*"

ROBERT BROWNING.

WATERLOO

On the eve of Waterloo a ball was held in Brussels which was attended by the Duke of Wellington and a number of officers belonging to the British army. Early next morning many of the soldiers left for the field of battle, among them being the Duke of Brunswick.

The writer of these bold and emphatic lines stood a few years afterwards on the spot where the conflict had raged most fiercely, and his thoughts turned thence to the scene of pleasure from which not a few of those who fell had come.

The verse is the Spenserian stanza—the stanza of "The Bower of Bliss"!

Stop!—for thy tread is on an Empire's dust!
An earthquake's spoil is sepulchred below!
Is the spot marked with no colossal bust?
Nor column trophied for triumphal show?
None;[1] but the moral's truth tells simpler so,
As the ground was before, thus let it be:—
How that red rain hath made the harvest grow!
And is this all the world has gained by thee,
Thou first and last of fields! king-making victory?

. . . . .

There was a sound of revelry by night,
And Belgium's capital had gathered then
Her Beauty and her Chivalry, and bright
The lamps shone o'er fair women and brave men;
A thousand hearts beat happily; and when
Music arose with its voluptuous swell
Soft eyes looked love to eyes which spake again,
And all went merry as a marriage bell;
But hush! hark! a deep sound strikes like a rising knell.

[1] These lines were written shortly after the battle: now a monument marks the place of the great contest.

Waterloo

Did ye not hear it ?—no : 'twas but the wind,
Or the car rattling o'er the stony street ;
On with the dance ! let joy be unconfined ;
No sleep till morn when Youth and Pleasure meet
To chase the glowing hours with flying feet—
But hark !—that heavy sound breaks in once more,
As if the clouds its echo would repeat ;
And nearer, clearer, deadlier than before !
<u>Arm ! arm ! it is—it is—the cannon's opening roar</u> !

Ah ! then and there was hurrying to and fro,
And gathering tears, and tremblings of distress,
And cheeks all pale which but an hour ago
Blushed at the praise of their own loveliness ;
And there were sudden partings, such as press
The life from out young hearts, and choking sighs
Which ne'er might be repeated ; who could guess
If ever more should meet those mutual eyes,
Since upon night so sweet such awful morn could rise.

And there was mounting in hot haste : the steed,
The mustering squadron, and the clattering car,
Went pouring forward with impetuous speed,
And swiftly forming in the ranks of war ;
And the deep thunder peal on peal afar ;

And, near, the beat of the alarming drum
Roused up the soldier ere the morning star,
While thronged the citizens with terror dumb,
Or whispering with white lips—" The foe.
     they come! they come!"

        .   .   .   .   .

And Ardennes waves above them her green
    leaves,
Dewy with nature's tear-drops as they pass,
Grieving, if aught inanimate e'er grieves,
Over the unreturning brave—alas,
E'er evening to be trodden like the grass
Which now beneath them, but above shall grow
In its next verdure, when this fiery mass
Of living valour, rolling on the foe
And burning with high hope, shall moulder cold
    and low.

Last noon beheld them full of lusty life,
Last eve in Beauty's circle proudly gay,
The midnight brought the signal-sound of
    strife,
The morn the marshalling in arms, the day
Battle's magnificently stern array!
The thunder-clouds close o'er it, which, when
    rent,
The earth is covered thick with other clay,
Which her own clay shall cover, heaped and
    pent,
Rider and horse,—friend, foe—in one red burial
    blent!

                              Lord Byron.

AGHADOE

There's a glade in Aghadoe, Aghadoe, Aghadoe,
    There's a green and silent glade in Aghadoe,
Where we met, my love and I, Love's fair planet in the sky,
    In that sweet and silent glade in Aghadoe.

There's a glen in Aghadoe, Aghadoe, Aghadoe,
    There's a deep and secret glen in Aghadoe,
Where I hid him from the eyes of the redcoats and their spies,
    That year the trouble came to Aghadoe.

O, my curse on one black heart in Aghadoe, Aghadoe,
    On Shaun Dhu, my mother's son in Aghadoe!
When your throat fries in hell's drouth, salt the flame be in your mouth,
    For the treachery you did in Aghadoe.

For they tracked me to that glen in Aghadoe, Aghadoe,
    When the price was on his head in Aghadoe:
O'er the mountain, by the wood, as I stole to him with food,
    Where in hiding lone he lay in Aghadoe.

But they never took him living in Aghadoe, Aghadoe;
    With the bullets in his heart in Aghadoe,
There he lay—the head my breast feels the warmth of where 'twould rest
    Gone, to win the traitor's gold, from Aghadoe.

But I walked to Mallow town from Aghadoe, Aghadoe,
  Brought his head from the gaol gate to Aghadoe ;
There I covered him with fern, and I piled on him the cairn ; *a heap of stones*
  Like an Irish king he sleeps in Aghadoe.

O, to creep into that cairn in Aghadoe, Aghadoe!
  There to rest upon his breast in Aghadoe!
Sure your dog for you could die with no truer heart than I,
  Your own love, cold on your cairn in Aghadoe.

John Todhunter.

III

MORNING

When the sweet morning, like a new-bathed child,
Comes running o'er the grass,
And all the wild
Leans out to see him pass;
'Tis then
The sun-kissed folk that are unseen of men,
From moon-enchanted meadows of the night
Haste to acclaim the light.
Where the smooth hill's high crest
With feathery groves is drest,
Their ancient altar stands.
Between the meshy leaves their white limbs glance
In immemorial dance;
I've glimpsed their hands
That part the coloured boughs to make
Pale flashing patterns in the dusky brake.

From " Bond and Free," by Evelyn Underhill.

ABT VOGLER

This is the reverie of a musician after he has been playing upon the organ, and a description of the music. Like " Childe Roland to the Dark Tower came," it admits us to the speaker's mind, in this case to his thoughts and feelings about his art.

Would that the structure brave, the manifold
    music I build,
Bidding my organ obey, calling its keys to their
    work,

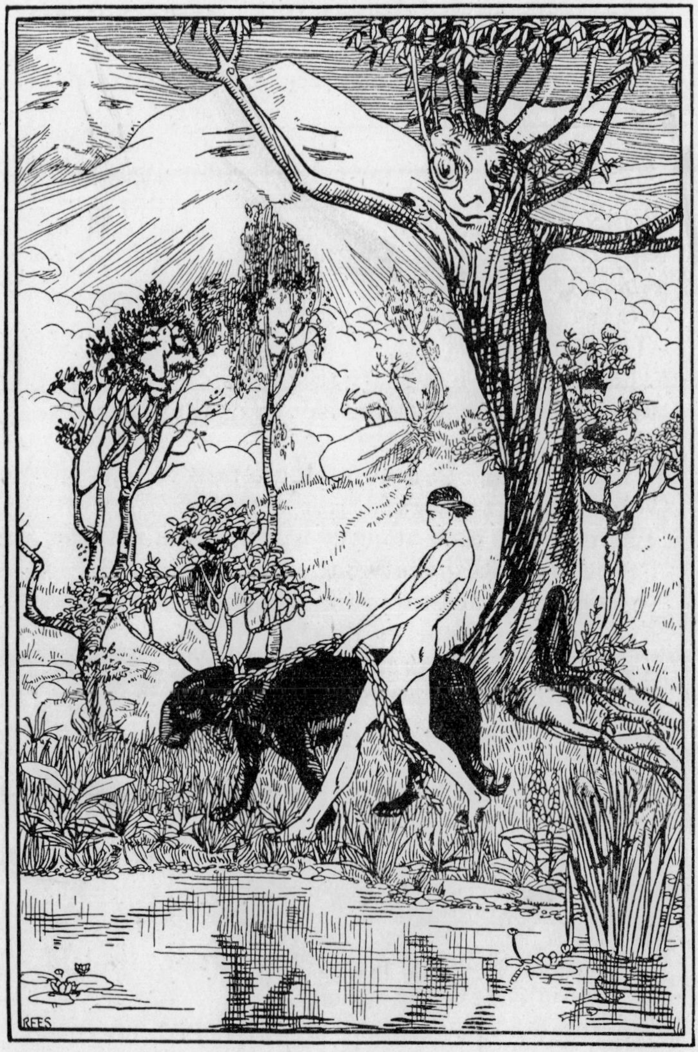
REES

Abt Vogler

Claiming each slave of the sound, at a touch, as when Solomon willed
Armies of angels that soar, legions of demons that lurk,
Man, brute, reptile, fly—alien of end and of aim,
Adverse, each from the other heaven-high, hell-deep removed—
Should rush into sight at once as he named the ineffable Name,
And pile him a palace straight, to pleasure the princess he loved!—

Would it might tarry like his, the beautiful building of mine,
This which my keys in a crowd pressed and importuned to raise!
Ah, one and all, how they helped, would dispart now and now combine,
Zealous to hasten the work, heighten their master his praise!
And one would bury his brow with a blind plunge down to hell,
Burrow awhile and build, broad on the roots of things,
Then up again swim into sight, having based me my palace well,
Founded it, fearless of flame, flat on the nether springs.

And another would mount and march, like the excellent minion he was,
Ay, another and yet another, one crowd but with many a crest,

Raising my rampired walls of gold as transparent as glass,
Eager to do and die, yield each his place to the rest:
For higher still and higher (as a runner tips with fire,
When a great illumination surprises a festal night,
Outlining round and round Rome's dome from space to spire)
Up, the pinnacled glory reached, and the pride of my soul was in sight.

In sight? Not half! for it seemed, it was certain, to match man's birth,
Nature in turn conceived, obeying an impulse as I;
And the emulous heaven yearned down, made effort to reach the earth,
As the earth had done her best, in my passion, to scale the sky:
Novel splendours burst forth, grew familiar and dwelt with mine,
Not a point, not a peak but found and fixed its wandering star;
Meteor-moons, balls of blaze: and they did not pale nor pine,
For earth had attained to heaven, there was no more near nor far.

Nay more: for there wanted not who walked in the glare and glow,
Presences plain in the place; or, fresh from the Protoplast,[1]

[1] The first creation.

Furnished for ages to come, when a kindlier wind
    should blow,
Lured now to begin and live, in a house to their
    liking at last ;
Or else the wonderful Dead who have passed
    through the body and gone,
But were back once more to breathe in an old
    world worth their new :
What never had been, was now ; what was, as it
    shall be anon ;
And what is—shall I say ?—matched both ; for
    I was made perfect too.

From " Abt Vogler," by Robert Browning.

KUBLA KHAN

    The author of " Kubla Khan " fell asleep in his chair at the moment when he was reading the following sentences in *Purchas His Pilgrimage* : " In Xamdu did Cublai Can build a stately Palace, encompassing sixteene miles of plaine ground with a wall, wherein are fertile meddowes, pleasant Springs, delightfull streames, and all sorts of beasts of chase and game, and in the middest thereof a sumptuous house of pleasure. . . . Hee for a superstitious feare suggested by his Astrologers, of a rebellion which sometime should bee raised against him in Cambalu, built a new Citie neere thereunto." It is interesting to compare these words with the dream-poem which was suggested by them.

In Xanadu did Kubla Khan
    A stately pleasure-dome decree,
Where Alph, the sacred river, ran
Through caverns measureless to man
    Down to a sunless sea.

So twice five miles of fertile ground
With walls and towers were girdled round:
And there were gardens bright with sinuous rills
Where blossomed many an incense-bearing tree;
And here were forests ancient as the hills,
Enfolding sunny spots of greenery.

But oh, that deep romantic chasm which slanted
Down the green hill athwart a cedarn cover!
A savage place! as holy and enchanted
As e'er beneath a waning moon was haunted
By woman wailing for her demon-lover!
And from this chasm, with ceaseless turmoil seething,
As if this earth in fast thick pants were breathing,
A mighty fountain momently was forced;
Amid whose swift half-intermittent burst
Huge fragments vaulted like rebounding hail,
Or chaffy grain beneath the thresher's flail:
And mid these dancing rocks at once and ever
It flung up momently the sacred river.
Five miles meandering with a mazy motion
Through wood and dale the sacred river ran,
Then reached the caverns measureless to man,
And sank in tumult to a lifeless ocean:
And mid this tumult Kubla heard from far
Ancestral voices prophesying war!

  The shadow of the dome of pleasure
    Floated midway on the waves;
  Where was heard the mingled measure
    From the fountain and the caves.
It was a miracle of rare device,
A sunny pleasure-dome with caves of ice!

A damsel with a dulcimer
  In a vision once I saw:
It was an Abyssinian maid,
  And on her dulcimer she played,
Singing of Mount Abora.
Could I revive with me
  Her symphony and song,
To such a deep delight 'twould win me,
That with music loud and long
I would build that dome in air,
That sunny dome! those caves of ice!
And all who heard should see them there,
And all should cry, "Beware! Beware!
His flashing eyes, his floating hair!
Weave a circle round him thrice,
  And close your eyes with holy dread;
  For he on honey-dew hath fed,
And drunk the milk of Paradise."

Samuel Taylor Coleridge.

FLANNAN ISLE

This grim story is told in a severely simple manner. The diction is almost bald; the metre is starkly plain; no effort is used to heighten the horror which the reader experiences; indeed, the effect on him is more tremendous because the tale is left almost entirely to produce its own "wonder all too dread for words." Step by step he is dragged to the empty room, "the door ajar, the untouched meal, and the over-toppled chair." Every detail of the picture possesses its own sinister meaning, and stands out clearly.

"Though three men dwell on Flannan Isle
To keep the lamp alight,
As we steered under the lee, we caught
No glimmer through the night!"

A passing ship at dawn had brought
The news; and quickly we set sail,
To find out what strange thing might ail
The keepers of the deep-sea light.

The winter day broke blue and bright,
With glancing sun and glancing spray,
As o'er the swell our boat made way,
As gallant as a gull in flight.

But, as we neared the lonely Isle,
And looked up at the naked height,
And saw the lighthouse towering white,
With blinded lantern, that all night
Had never shot a spark
Of comfort through the dark,
So ghostly in the cold sunlight
It seemed, that we were struck the while
With wonder all too dread for words.

And, as into the tiny creek
We stole beneath the hanging crag,
We saw three queer, black, ugly birds—
Too big, by far, in my belief,
For guillemot or shag—
Like seamen sitting bolt-upright
Upon a half-tide reef:
But, as we neared, they plunged from sight,
Without a sound, or spurt of white.

And, still too mazed to speak,
We landed; and made fast the boat;
And climbed the track in single file,
Each wishing he was safe afloat,

Flannan Isle

On any sea, however far,
So it be far from Flannan Isle:
And still we seemed to climb, and climb,
As though we'd lost all count of time,
And so must climb for evermore.
Yet, all too soon, we reached the door—
The black sun-blistered lighthouse door,
That gaped for us ajar.

As, on the threshold, for a spell
We paused, we seemed to breathe the smell
Of limewash and of tar,
Familiar as our daily breath,
As though 'twere some strange scent of death:
And so, yet wondering, side by side,
We stood a moment, still tongue-tied:
And each with black foreboding eyed
The door, ere we should fling it wide,
To leave the sunlight for the gloom:
Till, plucking courage up, at last,
Hard on each other's heels we passed
Into the living-room.

Yet, as we crowded through the door,
We only saw a table, spread
For dinner, meat and cheese and bread;
But all untouched; and no one there:
As though, when they sat down to eat,
Ere they could even taste,
Alarm had come; and they in haste
Had risen and left the bread and meat:
For at the table-head a chair
Lay tumbled on the floor.

We listened; but we only heard
The feeble chirping of a bird
That starved upon its perch:
And, listening still, without a word,
We set about our hopeless search.

We hunted high, we hunted low,
And soon ransacked the empty house;
Then o'er the Island, to and fro,
We ranged, to listen and to look
In every cranny, cleft, or nook
That might have hid a bird or mouse;
But, though we searched from shore to shore,
We found no sign in any place:
And soon again stood face to face
Before the gaping door:
And stole into the room once more
As frightened children steal.

Ay: though we hunted high and low,
And hunted everywhere,
Of the three men's fate we found no trace
Of any kind in any place,
But a door ajar, and an untouched meal,
And an overtoppled chair.

And as we listened in the gloom
Of that forsaken living-room—
A chill clutch on our breath—
We thought how ill-chance came to all
Who kept the Flannan Light:
And how the rock had been the death

Of many a likely lad :
How six had come to a sudden end
And three had gone stark mad :
And one whom we'd all known as friend
Had leapt from the lantern one still night,
And fallen by the lighthouse wall :
And long we thought
On the three we sought,
And of what might yet befall.

Like curs a glance has brought to heel,
We listened, flinching there :
And looked, and looked, on the untouched meal
And the overtoppled chair.

We seemed to stand for an endless while,
Though still no word was said :
Three men alive on Flannan Isle,
Who thought on three men dead.

Wilfrid Wilson Gibson.

KEITH OF RAVELSTON

Although in verse-form "Keith of Ravelston" is a ballad, its uncertain outline makes it quite different from the ordinary ballad; generally, a ballad tells a plain story, but in this poem the story is left to the reader's imagination.

THE murmur of the mourning ghost
    That keeps the shadowy kine :
"O Keith of Ravelston,
    The sorrows of thy line !"

Ravelston, Ravelston,
  The merry path that leads
Down the golden morning hill,
  And thro' the silver meads;

Ravelston, Ravelston,
  The stile beneath the tree,
The maid that kept her mother's kine,
  The song that sang she!

She sang her song, she kept her kine,
  She sat beneath the thorn,
When Andrew Keith of Ravelston
  Rode thro' the Monday morn.

His henchmen sing, his hawk-bells ring,
  His belted jewels shine:
O Keith of Ravelston,
  The sorrows of thy line!

. . . . .

Year after year, where Andrew came,
  Comes evening down the glade,
And still there sits a moonshine ghost
  Where sat the sunshine maid.

Her misty hair is faint and fair,
  She keeps her shadowy kine:
O Keith of Ravelston,
  The sorrows of thy line!

I lay my hand upon the stile,
  The stile is lone and cold,
The burnie that goes babbling by
  Says naught that can be told.

Yet, stranger, here from year to year,
  She keeps her shadowy kine:
O Keith of Ravelston
  The sorrows of thy line!

Step out three steps, where Andrew stood—
  Why blanch thy cheeks for fear?
The ancient stile is not alone,
  'Tis not the burn I hear!

She makes her immemorial moan,
  She keeps her shadowy kine:
O Keith of Ravelston,
  The sorrows of thy line!

Sydney Dobell.

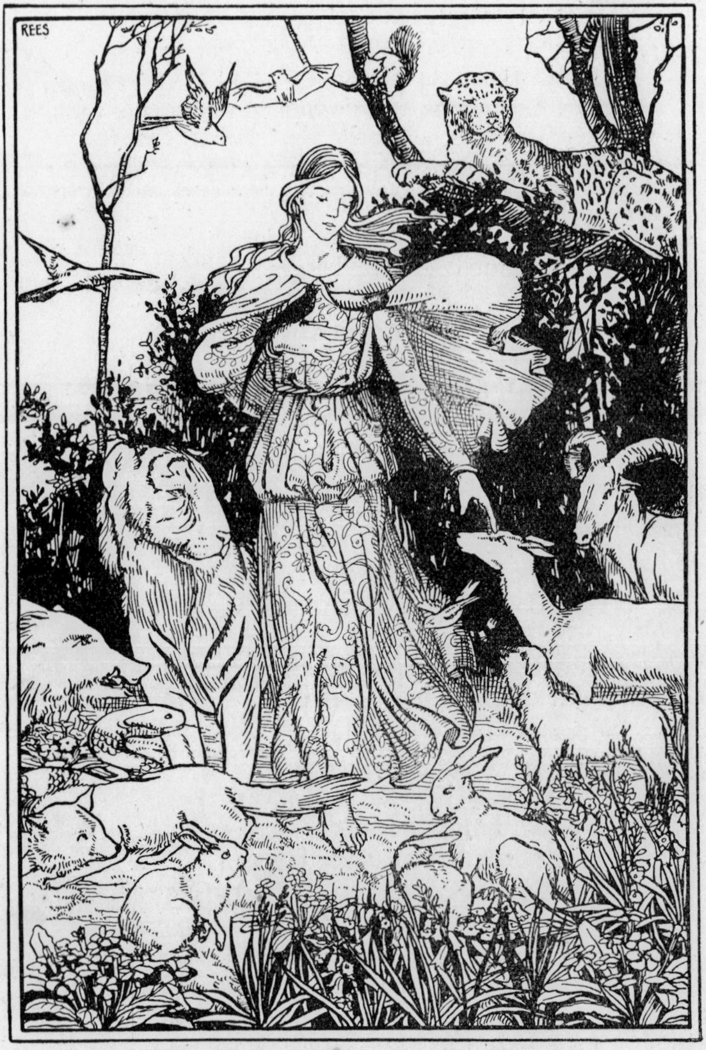
REES

IV
THE GARDEN

Sir Francis Bacon said that a garden is the purest of human pleasures. That remark is very well illustrated by this poem, which breathes purity and peace. Here there is no society, the busy trade of life does not vex, and time has no value. It is a poem of the open air, of sunlight, of green leaves and flowers, and of soft breezes.

How vainly men themselves amaze
To win the palm, the oak, or bays,
And their incessant labours see
Crowned from some single herb or tree,
Whose short and narrow-vergèd shade
Does prudently their toils upbraid ;
While all the flowers and trees do close
To weave the garlands of repose !

Fair Quiet, have I found thee here,
And Innocence, thy sister dear ?
Mistaken long, I sought you then
In busy companies of men :
Your sacred plants, if here below,
Only among the plants will grow :
Society is all but rude
To this delicious solitude.

No white nor red was ever seen
So amorous as this lovely green.
Fond lovers, cruel as their flame,
Cut in these trees their mistress' name :
Little, alas, they know or heed
How far these beauties hers exceed !
Fair trees, where'er your barks I wound,
No name shall but your own be found.

73

When we have run our passions' heat,
Love hither makes his best retreat:
The gods, that mortal beauty chase,
Still in a tree did end their race:
Apollo hunted Daphne so
Only that she might laurel grow;
And Pan did after Syrinx speed,
Not as a nymph, but for a reed.

What wondrous life is this I lead!
Ripe apples drop about my head;
The luscious clusters of the vine
Upon my mouth do crush their wine;
The nectarine and curious peach
Into my hands themselves do reach;
Stumbling on melons, as I pass,
Ensnared with flowers, I fall on grass.

Meanwhile the mind from pleasure less
Withdraws into its happiness;
The mind, that ocean where each kind
Does straight its own resemblance find;
Yet it creates, transcending these,
Far other worlds, and other seas,
Annihilating all that's made
To a green thought in a green shade.

There at the fountain's sliding foot,
Or at some fruit-tree's mossy root,
Casting the body's vest aside,
My soul into the boughs does glide;
There, like a bird, it sits and sings,
Then whets and combs its silver wings,

The Garden

And, till prepared for longer flight,
Waves in its plumes the various light.

Such was that happy garden-state
While man there walked without a mate;
After a place so pure and sweet
What other help could yet be meet?
But 'twas beyond a mortal's share
To wander solitary there:
Two paradises 'twere in one
To live in Paradise alone.

How well the skilful gardener drew
Of flowers and herbs this dial new!
Where, from above, the milder sun
Does through a fragrant zodiac run:
And, as it works, the industrious bee
Computes its time as well as we.
How could such sweet and wholesome hours
Be reckoned, but with herbs and flowers?

Andrew Marvell.

THE BOWER OF BLISS

Edmund Spenser has been called "The Poet's Poet" because he drew together so many of the means of poetic delight, and displayed so many of the resources of the poet's art. These verses are a riot of beautiful sights and sounds. The sweet smooth metre, the calm lingering stanza, and the massed images are all directed, most cleverly, to lull and charm, and to make with words an earthly paradise.

THERE the most dainty Paradise on ground
Itself doth offer to his sober eye,
In which all pleasures plenteously abound,
And none does other's happiness envỳ;

The painted flowers, the trees upshooting high,
The dales for shade, the hills for breathing-space,
The trembling groves, the crystal¹ running by,
And that which all fair works doth most aggrace,²
The art which all that wrought appearèd in no place.

Infinite streams continually did well
Out of a fountain, sweet and fair to see,
The which into an ample laver fell,
And shortly grew to so great quantity
That like a little lake it seemed to be;
Whose depth exceeded not three cubits' height,
That through the waves one might the bottom see,
All paved beneath with jasper shining bright,
That seemed the fountain in that sea did sail upright.

Eftsoons they heard a most melodious sound
Of all that mote³ delight a dainty ear,
Such as at once might not on living ground,
Save in the Paradise, be heard elsewhere:
Right hard it was for wight which did it hear
To read what manner music that mote be;
For all that pleasing is to living ear
Was there consorted in one harmony;
Birds, voices, instruments, winds, waters—all agreed.

The joyous birds, shrouded in cheerful shade,
Their notes unto the voice attempered sweet;

¹ Stream.   ² Adorn.   ³ Might.

The Bower of Bliss

Th' angelical soft trembling voices made
To th' instruments divine respondence meet;
The silver-sounding instruments did meet
With the bass murmur of the water's fall:
The water's fall, with difference discrete,
Now soft, now loud, unto the wind did call:
The gentle warbling wind low answerèd to all.

The whiles some one did chant this lovely lay:
"Ah! see, whoso fair thing dost fain to see,
In springing flower the image of thy day.
Ah! see the virgin Rose, how sweetly she
Doth first peep forth with bashful modesty,
That fairer seems the less ye see her may.
Lo! see soon after how more bold and free
Her barèd bosom she doth broad display;
Lo! see soon after how she fades, and falls away."
From "The Faerie Queene," by Edmund Spenser.

"THERE IS A HILL BESIDE THE SILVER THAMES"

This splendid piece is one of the best-known poems of the poet-laureate. It is equally distinguished for delight in nature, for the tenderness and truth of its descriptions, and for its excellent verse. In the last department, words made musical by alliteration and cunning assonance, pure rhymes, a beautiful stanza of the poet's own invention, choice and suitable epithets, and most skilful metre combine in a style which is perfectly married to its subject, and which, with the treatment of that subject, makes one of the masterpieces of English literature.

The quiet even tone suits perfectly the placidity of pastoral landscape; not for a word does it fail or falter.

THERE is a hill beside the silver Thames,
Shady with birch and beech and odorous pine:

And brilliant underfoot with thousand gems
Steeply the thickets to his floods decline.
   Straight trees in every place
   Their thick tops interlace,
And pendant branches trail their foliage fine
   Upon his watery face.

Swift from the sweltering pasturage he flows:
His stream, alert to seek the pleasant shade,
Pictures his gentle purpose, as he goes
Straight to the caverned pool his toil has made.
   His winter floods lay bare
   The stout roots in the air:
His summer streams are cool, when they have played
   Among their fibrous hair.

A rushy island guards this sacred bower,
And hides it from the meadow, where in peace
The lazy cows wrench many a scented flower,
Robbing the golden market of the bees:
   And laden barges float
   By banks of myosote;[1]
And scented flag and golden flower-de-lys
   Delay the loitering boat.

And on this side the island, where the pool
Eddies away, are tangled mass on mass
The water-weeds, that net the fishes cool,
And scarce allow a narrow stream to pass;
   Where spreading crowfoot mars
   The drowning nenuphars,[2]

[1] Forget-me-not.   [2] Water-lilies.

"There is a hill beside the silver Thames"

Waving the tassels of her silken grass
  Below her silver stars.

But in the purple pool there nothing grows,
Not the white water-lily spoked with gold;
Though best she loves the hollows, and well knows
On quiet streams her broad shields to unfold:
  Yet should her roots but try
  Within those deeps to lie,
Not her long reaching stalk could ever hold
  Her waxen head so high.

Sometimes an angler comes, and drops his hook
Within its hidden depths, and 'gainst a tree
Leaning his rod, reads in some pleasant book,
Forgetting soon his pride of fishery;
  And dreams, or falls asleep,
  While curious fishes peep
About his nibbled bait, or scornfully
  Dart off and rise and leap.

And sometimes a slow figure 'neath the trees,
In ancient-fashioned smock, with tottering care
Upon a staff propping his weary knees,
May by the pathway of the forest fare:
  As from a buried day
  Across the mind will stray
Some perishing mute shadow,—and unaware
  He passeth on his way.

Else, he that wishes solitude is safe,
Whether he bathe at morning in the stream;

Or lead his love there when the hot hours chafe
The meadows, busy with a blurring steam;
  Or watch, as fades the light,
  The gibbous[1] moon grow light
Until her magic rays dance in a dream,
  And glorify the night.

Where is this bower beside the silver Thames?
O pool and flowery thickets, hear my vow!
O trees of freshest foliage and straight stems,
No sharer of my secret I allow:
  Lest ere I come the while
  Strange feet your shades defile;
Or lest the burly oarsman turn his prow
  Within your guardian isle.

Robert Bridges.

THE BRIDGE

HERE, with one leap,
The bridge that spans the cutting; on its back
The load
Of the main-road,
And under it the railway track.

Into the plains they sweep,
Into the solitary plains asleep,
The flowing lines, the parallel lines of steel—
Fringed with their narrow grass,
Into the plains they pass,
The flowing lines, like arms of mute appeal.

[1] Almost at the full.

The Bridge

A cry
Prolonged across the earth—a call
To the remote horizons and the sky;
The whole east rushes down them with its light,
And the whole west receives them, with its pall
Of stars and night—
The flowing lines, the parallel lines of steel.

And with the fall
Of darkness, see! the red,
Bright anger of the signal, where it flares
Like a huge eye that stares
On some hid danger in the dark ahead.

A twang of wire—unseen
The signal drops; and, now instead
Of a red eye, a green.

Out of the silence grows
An iron thunder—grows, and roars, and sweeps,
Menacing! The plain
Suddenly leaps,
Startled, from its repose—
Alert and listening. Now, from the gloom
Of the soft distance, loom
Three lights, and over them, a brush
Of tawny flame and flying spark—
Three pointed lights that rush,
Monstrous, upon the cringing dark.

And nearer, nearer, rolls the sound,
Louder the throb and roar of wheels,
The shout of speed, the shriek of steam;
The sloping bank

Cut into flashing squares, gives back the clank
And grind of metal, while the ground
Shudders and the bridge reels—
As with a scream,
The train,
A rage of smoke, a laugh of fire,
A lighted anguish of desire,
A dream
Of gold and iron, of sound and flight,
Tumultuous roars across the night.

The train roars past—and, with a cry,
Drowned in a flying howl of wind,
Half-stifled in the smoke and blind,
The plain,
Shaken, exultant, unconfined,
Rises, flows on, and follows, and sweeps by,
Shrieking, to lose itself in distance and the sky.

John Redwood Anderson.

ODE TO AUTUMN

An inexhaustible storehouse of poetic treasures, the more this noble ode is contemplated the more various do its beauties appear. Although it is a picture in black and white—colour being absent from its imagery except in two lines of the last stanza—it is warm like the early autumn sun; and it has the magnificent opulence of harvest. It is also dignified and simple in structure; first comes the apostrophe, which is followed by elaborate personifications of Autumn, with the clearness of a series of woodcuts; lastly, under the quick fancy of the poet, the images change, and it is here that, with the songs of autumn, colour is introduced.

SEASON of mists and mellow fruitfulness!
  Close bosom-friend of the maturing sun;

Ode to Autumn

Conspiring with him how to load and bless
  With fruit the vines that round the thatch-eaves run ;
To bend with apples the mossed cottage-trees,
  And fill all fruit with ripeness to the core ;
    To swell the gourd, and plump the hazel-shells
With a sweet kernel : to set budding more,
And still more, later flowers for the bees,
Until they think warm days will never cease,
    For Summer has o'erbrimmed their clammy cells.—

Who hath not seen thee oft amid thy store ?
  Sometimes whoever seeks abroad may find
Thee sitting careless on a granary floor,
  Thy hair soft-lifted by the winnowing wind ;
Or on a half-reaped furrow sound asleep,
  Drowsed with the fume of poppies, while thy hook
    Spares the next swath and all its twinèd flowers ;
And sometimes like a gleaner thou dost keep
  Steady thy laden head across a brook ;
  Or by a cider-press, with patient look,
    Thou watchest the last oozings hours by hours.

Where are the songs of Spring ? Ay, where are they ?
  Think not of them, thou hast thy music too,—
While barrèd clouds bloom the soft-dying day,
  And touch the stubble-plains with rosy hue ;

Then in a wailful choir the small gnats mourn
　　Among the river sallows, borne aloft
　　　Or sinking as the light wind lives or dies;
And full-grown lambs loud bleat from hilly bourn;
　　Hedge-crickets sing; and now with treble soft
　　The redbreast whistles from a garden-croft,
　　　And gathering swallows twitter in the skies.

John Keats.

TO A SKYLARK

The "Ode to the Skylark" is a triumphant nature-song, a jubilant exclamation of delight over the beauty of the world, a series of rapturous images, each an attempt to symbolize the skylark's song, each partial and imperfect, but by its confessed imperfection exalting its subject. The ode reaches the height of lyrical achievement; it makes out of failure the greatest kind of success; its swift, clear, and confident music soars to heaven, as the skylark soars.

　　Hail to thee, blithe spirit!
　　　Bird thou never wert,
　　That from heaven or near it
　　　Pourest thy full heart
In profuse strains of unpremeditated art.

　　Higher still and higher
　　　From the earth thou springest
　　Like a cloud of fire;
　　　The blue deep thou wingest,
And singing still dost soar, and soaring ever singest.

　　In the golden lightning
　　　Of the sunken sun,
　　O'er which clouds are brightening,
　　　Thou dost float and run,
Like an unbodied joy whose race is just begun.

To a Skylark

4.
    The pale purple even
        Melts around thy flight;
   Like a star of heaven
      In the broad daylight
Thou art unseen, but yet I hear thy shrill delight,

5.
    Keen as are the arrows
       Of that silver sphere
   Whose intense lamp narrows
      In the white dawn clear
Until we hardly see, we feel that it is there.

6.
    All the earth and air
        With thy voice is loud,
   As, when night is bare,
      From one lonely cloud
The moon rains out her beams, and heaven is over-
      flowed.

7.
    What thou art we know not;
        What is most like thee?
   From rainbow clouds there flow not
      Drops so bright to see
As from thy presence showers a rain of melody:—

8.
    Like a poet hidden
        In the light of thought,
   Singing hymns unbidden,
      Till the world is wrought
To sympathy with hopes and fears it heeded not:

9.
    Like a high-born maiden
        In a palace tower,

    Soothing her love-laden
     Soul in secret hour
With music sweet as love, which overflows her bower :

    Like a glow-worm golden
     In a dell of dew,
    Scattering unbeholden
     Its aërial hue
Among the flowers and grass which screen it from the view :

    Like a rose embowered
     In its own green leaves,
    By warm winds deflowered,
     Till the scent it gives
Makes faint with too much sweet these heavy-wingèd thieves

    Sound of vernal showers
     On the twinkling grass,
    Rain-awakened flowers—
     All that ever was
Joyous and clear and fresh—thy music doth surpass.

    Teach us, sprite or bird,
     What sweet thoughts are thine :
    I have never heard
     Praise of love or wine
That panted forth a flood of rapture so divine.

    Chorus hymeneal
     Or triumphal chaunt,

To a Skylark

Matched with thine would be all
   But an empty vaunt—
A thing wherein we feel there is some hidden want.

15. What objects are the fountains
      Of thy happy strain?
   What fields, or waves, or mountains?
      What shapes of sky or plain?
   What love of thine own kind? What ignorance of pain?

16. With thy clear keen joyance,
      Languor cannot be:
   Shadow of annoyance
      Never came near thee:
   Thou lovest, but ne'er knew love's sad satiety.

17. Waking or asleep,
      Thou of death must deem
   Things more true and deep
      Than we mortals dream,
   Or how could thy notes flow in such a crystal stream?

18. We look before and after,
      And pine for what is not:
   Our sincerest laughter
      With some pain is fraught;
   Our sweetest songs are those that tell of saddest thought.

19. Yet, if we could scorn
      Hate, and pride, and fear,
   If we were things born
      Not to shed a tear,
   I know not how thy joy we ever should come near.

Better than all measures
   Of delightful sound,
Better than all treasures
   That in books are found,
Thy skill to poet were, thou scorner of the ground.

Teach me half the gladness
   That thy brain must know;
Such harmonious madness
   From my lips would flow,
The world should listen then, as I am listening now.

Percy Bysshe Shelley.

TO A MOUSE

ON TURNING HER UP IN HER NEST WITH THE PLOUGH, NOVEMBER 1785.

Wee, sleekit, cow'rin', tim'rous beastie,
O what a panic's in thy breastie!
Thou need na start awa sae hasty,
   Wi' bickering brattle [1]!
I wad be laith to rin and chase thee
   Wi' murd'ring pattle.[2]

I'm truly sorry Man's dominion
Has broken Nature's social union,
An' justifies that ill opinion
   Which makes thee startle
At me, thy poor earth-born companion,
   An' fellow mortal.

I doubt na, whiles,[3] but thou may thieve;
What then? Poor beastie, thou maun live.

[1] Hurry.   [2] Spade.   [3] Sometimes.

To a Mouse

A daimen-icker [1] in a thrave [2]
    'S a small request:
I'll get a blessing with the lave [3]
    And never miss 't.

Thy wee bit housie, too, in ruin!
It's silly wa's the win's are strewin,
An' naething, now, to big [4] a new ane,
    O foggage green!
An' bleak December's winds ensuin',
    Baith snell [5] an' keen!

Thou saw the fields laid bare and waste,
An' weary winter comin' fast,
An' cosy here, beneath the blast,
    Thou thought to dwell,
Till, crash! the cruel coulter past
    Out-thro thy cell.

That wee bit heap o' leaves an' stibble
Has cost thee mony a weary nibble.
Now thou's turned out, for a' thy trouble,
    But [6] house or hald,
To thole the winter's sleety dribble,
    An' cranreuch [7] cauld.

But, Mousie, thou art no thy lane
In proving foresight may be vain:
The best-laid schemes o' mice an' men
    Gang aft agley,
An' leave us nought but grief an' pain
    For promised joy.

[1] Occasional ear of corn.
[2] Rick.
[3] Remainder.
[4] Build.
[5] Biting.
[6] Without.
[7] Hoarfrost.

Still thou art blest compared wi' me;
The present only toucheth thee:
But oh, I backward cast my e'e
    On prospects drear,
An' forward tho' I canna see,
    I guess an' fear.

Robert Burns.

LINES WRITTEN IN EARLY SPRING

Keats's "Ode to Autumn" and Wordsworth's "Lines written in Early Spring" are both nature poems, but are quite unlike. The former is a pure description of its subject, while this penetrates, through nature, to the spirit behind nature. The loveliness of nature, according to Wordsworth, is the means by which that spirit speaks to man, and influences him. Further, the poet felt very strongly the contrast between the purity of nature and the imperfections into which, he believed, man has allowed himself to fall. The influence of nature upon man, according to him, is to elevate and refine the human spirit.

I heard a thousand blended notes
While in a grove I sate reclined,
In that sweet mood when pleasant thoughts
Bring sad thoughts to the mind.

To her fair works did Nature link
The human soul that through me ran;
And much it grieved my heart to think
What Man has made of Man.

Through primrose tufts, in that green bower,
The periwinkle trailed its wreaths;
And 'tis my faith that every flower
Enjoys the air it breathes.

The birds around me hopped and played;
Their thoughts I cannot measure,
But the least motion that they made,
It seemed a thrill of pleasure.

The budding twigs spread out their fan
To catch the breezy air;
And I must think, do all I can,
That there was pleasure there.

If this belief from heaven be sent,
If such be Nature's holy plan,
Have I not reason to lament
What Man has made of Man?
                    William Wordsworth.

UPON WESTMINSTER BRIDGE, SEPTEMBER 3, 1802

EARTH has not anything to show more fair;
Dull would he be of soul who could pass by
A sight so touching in its majesty:
This City now doth like a garment wear
The beauty of the morning: silent, bare,
Ships, towers, domes, theatres, and temples lie
Open unto the fields, and to the sky,
All bright and glittering in the smokeless air.
Never did sun more beautifully steep
In his first splendour valley, rock, or hill;
Ne'er saw I, never felt, a calm so deep.
The river glideth at his own sweet will:
Dear God! the very houses seem asleep,
And all that mighty heart is lying still.
                    William Wordsworth.

THE MUSIC OF THE SPHERES

Until the time of Shakespeare Englishmen retained the belief that all the planets and heavenly bodies revolved round the earth; and poets cherished the beautiful fancy—it can scarcely be said to have been a belief—that each planet, as it moved, emitted a musical sound, the whole set of notes composing a harmony which is the silence of the starry sky.

    Look how the floor of heaven
Is thick inlaid with patines of bright gold:
There's not the smallest orb that thou behold'st
But in his motion like an angel sings,
  Still quiring to the young-eyed cherubins;
Such harmony is in immortal souls;
But, whilst this muddy vesture of decay
Doth grossly close it in, we cannot hear it.
                 William Shakespeare.

V

AMPHION

According to ancient story, the god Apollo endowed Amphion with such skill in music that, when he played, he could charm wild beasts, move trees, and cause building-stones to arrange themselves in the places designed for them. The poet takes this idea and gives it a modern application, drawing from it, in conclusion, a little moral.

My father left a park to me,
  But it is wild and barren,
A garden too with scarce a tree
  And waster than a warren:
Yet say the neighbours when they call,
  It is not bad but good land,
And in it is the germ of all
  That grows within the woodland.

Oh, had I lived when song was great
  In days of old Amphion,
And ta'en my fiddle to the gate,
  Nor cared for seed nor scion!
And had I lived when song was great
  And legs of trees were limber,
And ta'en my fiddle to the gate,
  And fiddled in the timber!

'Tis said he had a tuneful tongue,
  Such happy intonation,
Wherever he sat down and sung,
  He left a small plantation:
Wherever in some lonely grove
  He set up his forlorn pipes,
The gouty oaks began to move
  And flounder into hornpipes.

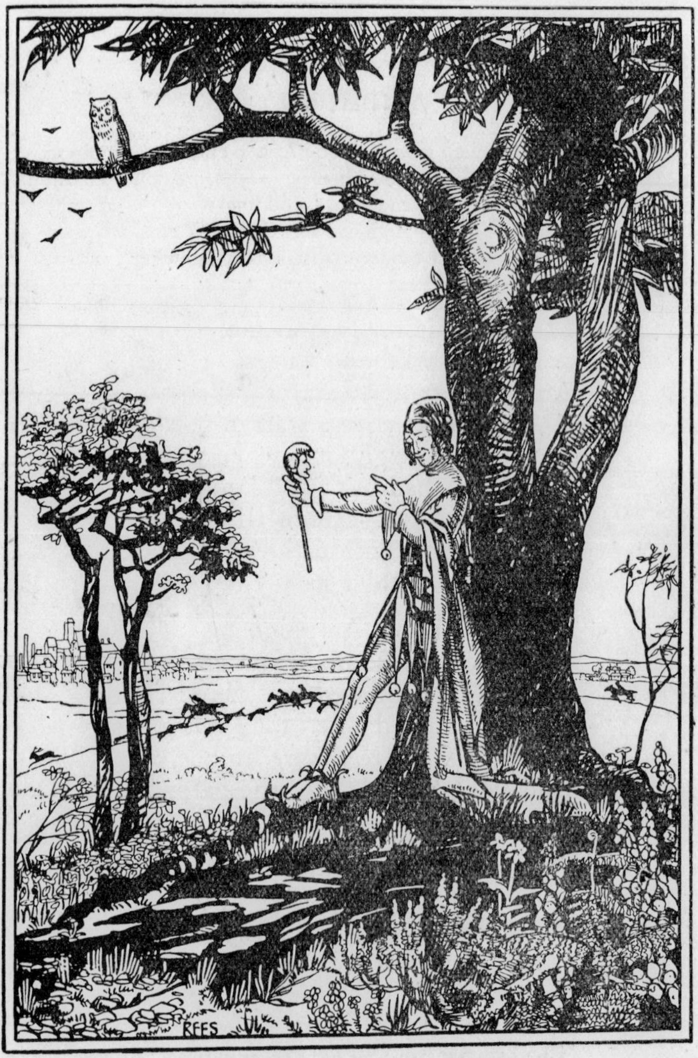
REES

Amphion

The mountain stirred its bushy crown,
    And, as tradition teaches,
Young ashes pirouetted down
    Coquetting with young beeches;
And briony-vine and ivy wreath
    Ran forward to his rhyming,
And from the valleys underneath
    Came little copses climbing.

The linden broke her ranks and rent
    The ivy-wreaths that bind her,
And down the middle, buzz! she went
    With all her bees behind her:
The poplars, in long order due,
    With cypress promenaded,
The shock-head willows two and two
    By rivers gallopaded.

Came wet-shod alder from the wave,
    Came yews, a dismal coterie;
Each plucked his one foot from the grave
    Poussetting with a sloe-tree;
Old elms came breaking from the vine,
    The vine streamed out to follow,
And, sweating rosin, plumped the pine
    From many a cloudy hollow.

And wasn't it a sight to see,
    When, ere his song was ended,
Like some great landslip, tree by tree
    The countryside descended:
And shepherds from the mountain-eaves
    Looked down, half-pleased, half-frightened,
As dashed about the drunken leaves
    The random sunshine lightened!

Oh, nature first was fresh to men,
    And wanton without measure;
So youthful and so flexile then,
    You moved her at your pleasure.
Twang out, my fiddle! Shake the twigs!
    And make her dance attendance;
Blow, flute, and stir the stiff-set sprigs,
    And scirrhous roots and tendons.

'Tis vain! in such a brassy age
    I could not move a thistle;
The very sparrows in the hedge
    Scarce answer to my whistle;
Or at the most, when three-parts-sick
    With strumming and with scraping,
A jackass heehaws from the rick,
    The passive oxen gaping.

But what is that I hear? a sound
    Like sleepy counsel pleading;
O Lord!—'tis in my neighbour's ground,
    The modern Muses reading.
They read Botanic treatises
    And Works on Gardening through there,
And Methods of Transplanting Trees
    To look as if they grew there.

The withered Misses! how they prose
    O'er books of travelled seamen,
And show you slips of all that grows
    From England to Van Diemen.
They read in arbours clipt and cut,
    And alleys, faded places,
By squares of tropic summer shut
    And warmed in crystal cases.

Amphion

But these, tho' fed with careful dirt,
   Are neither green nor sappy;
Half-conscious of the garden squirt,
   The spindlings look unhappy.
Better to me the meanest weed
   That blows upon its mountain,
The vilest herb that runs to seed
   Beside its native fountain.

And I must work thro' months of toil,
   And years of cultivation,
Upon my proper patch of soil
   To grow my own plantation.
I'll take the showers as they fall,
   I will not vex my bosom:
Enough if at the end of all
   A little garden blossom.

Lord Tennyson.

THE VICAR OF BRAY

English poetry contains a good deal of verse of the kind that is called Satire: "The Vicar of Bray" is a satire upon those who, in the troublous times of the latter half of the seventeenth century, changed their opinions with every change of government.

In good King Charles' golden days,
   When loyalty no harm meant,
A zealous High Church man was I,
   And so I got preferment.
To teach my flock I never missed
   Kings were by God appointed,
And damned are those who dare resist
   Or touch the Lord's anointed.

And this is law that I'll maintain
    Until my dying day, sir,
That whatsoever king shall reign,
    I'll still be the Vicar of Bray, sir.

When royal James obtained the throne,
    And Popery came in fashion,
The penal laws I hooted down,
    And read the Declaration.
The Church of Rome I found would fit
    Full well my constitution,
And had become a Jesuit
    But for the Revolution.

When William was our king declared,
    To ease the nation's grievance,
With the new crowd about I steered,
    And swore to him allegiance;
Old principles I did revoke,
    Set conscience at a distance,
Passive obedience was a joke,
    A jest was non-resistance.

When gracious Anne became our Queen,
    The Church of England's glory,
Another face of things was seen,
    And I became a Tory.
Occasional Conformists base—
    I damned their moderation,
And thought the Church in danger was
    By such prevarication.

When George in pudding-time came o'er,
    And moderate men looked big, sir,

I turned a cat-in-pan once more,
　And so became a Whig, sir;
And thus preferment I procured
　From our new faith's defender,
And almost every day abjured
　The Pope and the Pretender.

The illustrious house of Hanover,
　And Protestant succession,
To these I do allegiance swear,—
　While they can keep possession.
For in my faith and loyalty
　I never more will falter,
And George my lawful king shall be,—
　Until the times do alter.

　　　　　　　　Anonymous.

MacFLECKNOE

"MacFlecknoe" is a satire upon a poet named Shadwell. Flecknoe was a poet of the preceding generation who was known for the poor quality of his writings, and Dryden calls Shadwell his intellectual son. The piece is too absurd to be really ill-natured: it has a comic effect that is due to intentional exaggeration. Point is given to its sarcasms by the style of the verse in which it is written, each couplet being like a fresh stab. We care no longer for Flecknoe and Shadwell, but this savagely-delicious satire is beyond the touch of Time.

ALL human things are subject to decay,
And, when Fate summons, monarchs must obey.
This Flecknoe found, who, like Augustus, young
Was called to empire and had governed long;
In prose and verse was owned without dispute
Through all the realms of nonsense absolute.

This aged prince, now flourishing in peace,
And blest with issue of a large increase,
Worn out with business, did at length debate
To settle the succession of the state;
And pondering which of all his sons was fit
To reign and wage immortal war with wit,
Cried, " 'Tis resolved, for Nature pleads that he
Should only reign who most resembles me.
Shadwell alone my perfect image bears,
Mature in dulness from his tender years;
Shadwell alone, of all my sons, is he
Who stands confirmed in full stupidity.
The rest to some faint meaning make pretence,
But Shadwell never deviates into sense.
Some beams of wit on other souls may fall,
Strike through, and make a lucid interval;
But Shadwell's genuine night admits no ray,
His rising fogs prevail upon the day——"
Here stopped the good old sire, and wept for joy
In silent raptures of the hopeful boy.

John Dryden.

THE BALLAD OF BEAU BROCADE

I

SEVENTEEN hundred and thirty-nine:—
That was the date of this tale of mine.

First great GEORGE was buried and gone;
GEORGE the Second was plodding on.

LONDON then, as the "Guides" aver,
Shared its glories with *Westminster*;

The Ballad of Beau Brocade

And people of rank, to correct their "tone,"
Went out of town to *Marybone*.

Those were the days of the War with *Spain*,
PORTO-BELLO would soon be ta'en;

WHITEFIELD preached to the colliers grim,
Bishops in lawn sleeves preached at him;

WALPOLE talked of "a man and his price";
Nobody's virtue was over-nice:—

Those, in fine, were the brave days when
Coaches were stopped by . . . *Highwaymen*!

And of all the knights of the gentle trade
Nobody bolder than "BEAU BROCADE."

This they knew on the whole way down;
Best,—maybe,—at the "*Oak and Crown.*"

(For timorous cits on their pilgrimage
Would "club" for a "Guard" to ride the stage;

And the Guard that rode on more than one
Was the Host of this hostel's sister's son.)

Open we here on a March day fine,
Under the oak with the hanging sign.

There was Barber DICK with his basin by;
Cobbler JOE with the patch on his eye;

Portly product of Beef and Beer,
JOHN the host, he was standing near.

Straining and creaking, with wheels awry
Lumbering came the "*Plymouth Fly*";—

Lumbering up from *Bagshot Heath*,
Guard in the basket armed to the teeth;

Passengers heavily armed inside;
Not the less surely the coach had been tried!

Tried!—but a couple of miles away,
By a well-dressed man!—in the open day!

Tried successfully, never a doubt,—
Pockets of passengers all turned out!

Cloak-bags rifled, and cushions ripped,—
Even an Ensign's wallet stripped.

Even a Methodist hosier's wife
Offered the choice of her Money or Life!

Highwayman's manners no less polite,
Hoped that their coppers (returned) were right:—

Sorry to find the company poor,
Hoped next time they'd travel with more;—

Plucked them all at his ease, in short:—
Such was the "*Plymouth Fly's*" report.

Sympathy! horror! and wonderment!
"Catch the villain!" (But nobody went.)

Hosier's wife led into the Bar;
(That's where the best strong waters are!)

The Ballad of Beau Brocade

Followed the tale of the hundred-and-one
Things that Somebody ought to have done.

Ensign (of BRAGG's) made a terrible clangour:
But for the Ladies had drawn his hanger!

Robber, of course, was " BEAU BROCADE ";
Out-spoke DOLLY the Chambermaid.

Devonshire DOLLY, plump and red,
Spoke from the gallery overhead;—

Spoke it out boldly, staring hard:—
" Why didn't you shoot, then, GEORGE the
    Guard?"

Spoke it out bolder, seeing him mute:—
" GEORGE the Guard, why didn't you shoot?"

Portly JOHN grew pale and red,
(JOHN was afraid of her, people said;)

Gasped that " DOLLY was surely cracked,"
(JOHN was afraid of her—that's a fact!)

GEORGE the Guard grew red and pale,
Slowly finished his quart of ale:—

" Shoot? Why — Rabbit him! — didn't he
    shoot?"
Muttered—" The Baggage was far too 'cute!"

" Shoot? Why, he'd flashed the pan in his eye!"
Muttered—" She'd pay for it by and by!"
Further than this made no reply.

Nor could a further reply be made,
For GEORGE *was in league with* " BEAU BROCADE " !

And JOHN the Host, in his wakefullest state,
Was not—on the whole—immaculate.

But nobody's virtue was over-nice
When WALPOLE talked of " a man and his price " ;

And wherever Purity found abode,
'Twas certainly *not* on a posting road.

II

" Forty " followed to " Thirty-nine."
Glorious days of the *Hanover* line !

Princes were born, and drums were banged ;
Now and then batches of Highwaymen hanged.

" Glorious news ! " from the *Spanish Main* ;
PORTO-BELLO at last was ta'en.

" Glorious news ! "—for the liquor trade ;
Nobody dreamed of " BEAU BROCADE."

People were thinking of *Spanish Crowns* ;
Money was coming from seaport towns !

Nobody dreamed of " BEAU BROCADE,"
(Only DOLLY the Chambermaid !).

Blessings on VERNON ! Fill up the cans ;
Money was coming in " *Flys* " and " *Vans*."

The Ballad of Beau Brocade

Possibly, JOHN the Host had heard;
Also, certainly, GEORGE the Guard.

And DOLLY had possibly tidings, too,
That made her rise from her bed anew,

Plump as ever, but stern of eye,
With a fixed intention to warn the " *Fly*."

Lingering only at JOHN his door,
Just to make sure of a jerky snore;

Saddling the grey mare, *Dumpling Star*;
Fetching the pistol out of the bar;

(The old horse-pistol that, they say,
Came from the battle of *Malplaquet*;)

Loading with powder that maids would use,
Even in " Forty," to clear the flues;

And a couple of silver buttons the Squire
Gave her, away in *Devonshire*.

These she wadded—for want of a better—
With the B-SH-P of L-ND-N's " Pastoral Letter ";

Looked to the flint, and hung the whole,
Ready to use, at her pocket-hole.

Thus equipped and accoutred, DOLLY
Clattered away to " *Exciseman's Folly* ";—

Such was the name of a ruined abode
Just on the edge of the *London* road.

Thence she thought she might safely try,
As soon as she saw it, to warn the "*Fly*."

But, as chance fell out, her rein she drew,
As the BEAU came cantering into the view.

By the light of the moon she could see him drest
In his famous gold-sprigged tambour vest;

And under his silver-gray surtout
The laced, historical coat of blue,

That he wore when he went to *London-Spaw*,
And robbed SIR MUNGO MUCKLETHRAW.

Out-spoke DOLLY the Chambermaid,
(Trembling a little, but not afraid,)
" Stand and Deliver, O ' BEAU BROCADE ' ! "

But the BEAU rode nearer, and would not speak,
For he saw by the moonlight a rosy cheek;

And a spavined mare with a rusty hide,
And a girl with her hand at her pocket-side.

So never a word he spoke as yet,
For he thought 'twas a freak of MEG or BET;—
A freak of the " *Rose* " or the " *Rummer* " set.

Out-spoke DOLLY the Chambermaid,
(Tremulous now, and sore afraid,)
" Stand and Deliver, O ' BEAU BROCADE ' ! "—

Firing then, out of sheer alarm,
Hit the BEAU in the bridle-arm.

The Ballad of Beau Brocade

Button the first went none knows where,
But it carried away his *solitaire* ;

Button the second a circuit made,
Glanced in under the shoulder-blade ;—
Down from the saddle fell " BEAU BROCADE "!

Down from the saddle and never stirred !—
DOLLY grew white as a *Windsor* curd.

Slipped not less from the mare, and bound
Strips of her kirtle about his wound.

Then, lest his Worship should rise and flee,
Fettered his ankles—tenderly.

Jumped on his chestnut, BET the fleet
(Called after BET of *Portugal Street*) ;

Came like the wind to the old Inn-door ;—
Roused fat JOHN from a three-fold snore ;—

Vowed she'd 'peach if he misbehaved . . .
Briefly, the " *Plymouth Fly* " was saved !

Staines and *Windsor* were all on fire :—
DOLLY was wed to a *Yorkshire* squire ;
Went to town at the K—G's desire !

But, whether his M—J—STY saw her or not,
HOGARTH jotted her down on the spot ;

And something of DOLLY one still may trace
In the fresh contours of his " *Milkmaid's* " face.

GEORGE the Guard fled over the sea :
JOHN had a fit—of perplexity ;

Turned King's evidence, sad to state :—
But JOHN was never immaculate.

As for the BEAU, he was duly tried,
When his wound was healed, at *Whitsuntide* ;

Served—for a day—as the last of " sights,"
To the world of *St. James's-Street* and " *White's*,"

Went on his way to TYBURN TREE,
With a pomp befitting his high degree.

Every privilege rank confers :—
Bouquet of pinks at *St. Sepulchre's* ;

Flagon of ale at *Holborn Bar* ;
Friends (in mourning) to follow his Car—
(" t " is omitted where HEROES are !)

Everyone knows the speech he made ;
Swore that he " rather admired the Jade " !—

Waved to the crowd with his gold-laced hat ;
Talked to the chaplain after that ;

Turned to the Topsman undismayed . . .
This was the finish of " BEAU BROCADE " !

And this is the Ballad that seemed to hide
In the leaves of a dusty " LONDONER'S GUIDE " ;

"*Humbling Inscrib'd (with curls and tails)
By the Author to* FREDERICK, *Prince of* WALES :—

"*Published by* FRANCIS *and* OLIVER PINE ;
*Ludgate-Hill, at the Blackmoor Sign.
Seventeen-Hundred-and-Thirty-Nine.*"
                                        Austin Dobson.

THE SOCIETY UPON THE STANISLAUS

I RESIDE at Table Mountain, and my name is
    Truthful James ;
I am not up to small deceit, or any sinful games ;
And I'll tell in simple language what I know about
    the row
That broke up our society upon the Stanislow.

But first I would remark, that it's not a proper
    plan
For any scientific gent to whale his fellow-man ;
And, if a member don't agree with his peculiar
    whim,
To lay for that same member for to " put a head "
    on him.

Now nothing could be finer or more beautiful to
    see
Than the first six months' proceedings of that
    same society,
Till Brown of Calaveras brought a lot of fossil
    bones
That he found within a tunnel near the tenement
    of Jones.

Then Brown he read a paper, and he reconstructed there,
From those same bones, an animal that was extremely rare;
And Jones then asked the Chair for a suspension of the rules,
Till he could prove that those same bones was one of his lost mules.

Then Brown he smiled a bitter smile, and said he was at fault,
It seemed he had been trespassing on Jones's family vault;
He was a most sarcastic man, this quiet Mr. Brown,
And on several occasions he had cleaned out the town.

Now I hold it is not decent for a scientific gent
To say another is an ass,—at least, to all intent;
Nor should the individual who happens to be meant
Reply by heaving rocks at him—to any great extent.

Then Abner Dean of Angel's raised a point of order—when
A chunk of Old Red Sandstone took him in the abdomen,
And he smiled a sickly kind of smile, and curled up on the floor,
And the subsequent proceedings interested him no more.

For in less time than I write it, every member did engage
In a warfare with the remains of a Palæozoic Age;

The Society upon the Stanislaus   111

And the way they heaved those fossils in their
    anger was a sin,
Till the skull of an old mammoth caved the head
    of Thomson in.

And this is all I have to say of these improper
    games,
For I live at Table Mountain, and my name is
    Truthful James;
And I've told in simple language what I know
    about the row
That broke up our society upon the Stanislow.
                    F. Bret Harte.

DUNCAN GRAY

Duncan Gray cam here to woo,
    Ha, ha, the wooing o't;
On blithe Yule night when we were fou,[1]
    Ha, ha, the wooing o't:
Maggie coost her head fu' high,
Looked asklent[2] and unco skeigh,[3]
Gart[4] poor Duncan stand abeigh[5];
    Ha, ha, the wooing o't.

Duncan fleeched,[6] and Duncan prayed;
Meg was deaf as Ailsa Craig;
Duncan sighed baith out and in,
Grat[7] his een baith bleer't and blin',
Spak o' lowpin' ower a linn![8]

    [1] Merry.   [5] Aloof.
    [2] Aside.   [6] Begged.
    [3] Very disdainful.   [7] Wept.
    [4] Made.   [8] Waterfall.

Time and chance are but a tide,
Slighted love is sair to bide;
Shall I, like a fule, quoth he,
For a haughty hizzie dee?
She may gae to—France for me!

How it comes let doctors tell.
Meg grew sick—as he grew well;
Something in her bosom wrings,
For relief a sigh she brings;
And O, her een, they spak such things!

Duncan was a lad o' grace;
Maggie's was a piteous case;
Duncan couldna be her death,
Swelling pity smoored his wrath;
Now they're crouse and canty baith :[1]
    Ha, ha, the wooing o't!

Robert Burns.

MUIOPOTMOS

Of all the race of silver-wingèd flies
Which do possess the empire of the air,
Betwixt the centred earth and azure skies,
Was none more favourable nor more fair,
Whilst heaven did favour his felicities,
Than Clarion, the eldest son and heir
Of Muscaroll, and in his father's sight
Of all alive did seem the fairest wight.

For he so swift and nimble was of flight
That from this lower tract he dared to sty [2]

---

[1] Now they're both brisk and lively.   [2] Soar.

Muiopotmos 113

Up to the clouds, and thence with pinions light
To mount aloft unto the crystal sky,
To view the workmanship of heaven's height:
Whence down descending he along would fly
Upon the streaming rivers, sport to find;
And oft would dare to tempt the troublous wind.

So on a summer's day, when season mild
With gentle calm the world had quieted,
And high in heaven Hyperion's fiery child,
Ascending, did his beams abroad dispread,
Whiles all the heavens on lower creatures smiled,
Young Clarion with vauntful lustihead
After his guize [1] did cast abroad to fare,
And thereto gan his furnitures [2] prepare.

His breastplate first, that was of substance pure,
Before his noble heart he firmly bound,
That mought [3] his heart from iron death assure,
And ward his gentle corpse from cruel wound:
For it by art was framed to endure
The bite of baleful steel and bitter stound [4]
No less than that which Vulcan made to shield
Achilles' life from fate of Troyan field.

And then about his shoulders broad he threw
An hairy hide of some wild beast whom he
In savage forest by adventure slew,
And reft the spoil his ornament to be;
Which spreading all his back with dreadful view
Made all that him so horrible did see
Think him Alcides with the lion's skin,
When the Nemean conquest he did win.

[1] According to his wont.
[2] Armour.
[3] Could.
[4] Combat.

114 *A Book of English Poems*

Upon his head his glistening burganet,
The which was wrought by wonderous device,
And curiously engraven, he did set:
The metal was of rare and passing price;
Not Bilbo steel, nor brass from Corinth fet,
Nor costly Oricalche from strange Phœnice,
But such as could both Phœbus' arrows ward,
And the hailing darts of heaven beating hard.

Therein two deadly weapons fixed he bore,
Strongly outlancèd towards either side,
Like two sharp spears, his enemies to gore:
Like as a warlike brigantine, applied
To fight, lays forth her threatful pikes afore
The engines which in them sad death do hide,
So did this fly outstretch his fearful horns,
Yet so as him their terror more adorns.

Lastly his shiny wings as silver bright,
Painted with thousand colours, passing far
All painter's skill, he did about him dight:
Not half so many sundry colours are
In Iris' bow, ne heaven doth shine so bright,
Distinguishèd with many a twinkling star,
Nor Juno's bird in her eye-spotted train
So many goodly colours doth contain.

Thus the fresh Clarion being ready dight
Unto his journey did himself address,
And with good speed began to take his flight
Over the fields in his frank lustiness,
And all the champain he soarèd light,
And all the country wide he did possess,
Feeding upon their pleasures bounteously,
That none gainsaid, nor none did him envỳ.

Muiopotmos

To the gay gardens his unstaid desire
Him wholly carried, to refresh his sprites.
There lavish Nature in her best attire
Pours forth sweet odours and alluring sights,
And Art, with her contending, doth aspire
To excel the natural with made delights;
And all that fair or pleasant may be found
In riotous excess doth there abound.

There he arriving round about doth fly
From bed to bed, from one to other border,
And takes survey with curious busy eye,
Of every flower and herb there set in order;
Now this, now that, he tasteth tenderly,
Yet none of them he rudely doth disorder,
Ne with his feet their silken leaves deface,
But pastures on the pleasures of each place.

But what on earth can long abide in state?
Or who can him assure of happy day,
Sith [1] morning fair may bring foul evening late,
And least mishap the most bliss alter may?
For thousand perils lie in close await
About us daily, to work our decay,
That none, except a God, or God him guide,
May them avoid or remedy provide.

It fortunèd (as heavens had behight [2])
That in this garden, where young Clarion
Was wont to solace him, a wicked wight,
The foe of fair things, the author of confusion,
The shame of Nature, the bondslave of spite,
Had lately built his hateful mansion,

[1] Since. [2] Ordained.

And, lurking closely, in await now lay,
How he might any in his trap betray.

This cursed creature, mindful of that old
Infestered grudge the which his mother felt,
So soon as Clarion he did behold,
His heart with vengeful malice inly swelt;
And, weaving straight a net with many a fold
About the cave in which he lurking dwelt,
With fine small cords about it stretchèd wide,
So finely spun that scarce they could be spied.

Who now shall give unto my heavy eyes
A well of tears, that all may overflow?
Or where shall I find lamentable cries
And mournful runes enough my grief to show?
Help, O thou Tragic Muse, me to devise
Notes sad enough to express this bitter throe;
For lo, the dreary stound is now arrived
That of all happiness hath us deprived.

The luckless Clarion, whether cruel Fate,
Or wicked Fortune faultless him misled,
Or some ungracious blast out of the gate
Of Æol's reign [1] perforce him drove on head,
Was (O, sad hap and hour unfortunate!)
With violent swift flight forth carrièd
Into the cursed cobweb which his foe
Had framèd for his final overthrow.

There the fond [2] fly entangled, struggled long
Himself to free thereout, but all in vain;
For striving more the more in laces strong
Himself he tied, and wrapt wingès twain

[1] Kingdom.   [2] Foolish.

Muiopotmos

In limy snares the subtle loops among,
That in the end he breathless did remain,
And, all his youthly forces idly spent,
Him to the mercy of the avenger lent.

Which when the grisly tyrant did espy,
Like a grim lion rushing with fierce might
Out of his den, he seizèd greedily
On the resistless prey, and with fell spite
Under the left wing struck his weapon sly
Into his heart, that his deep-groaning sprite
In bloody streams forth fled into the air,
His body left the spectacle of care.

Edmund Spenser.

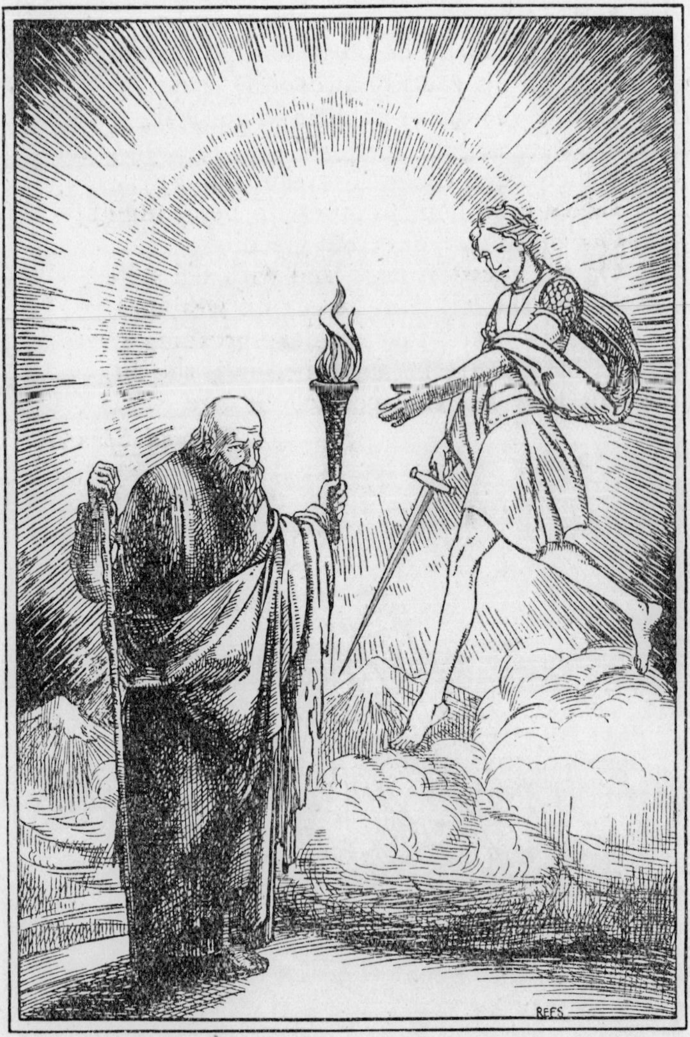
REES

VI

"FULL MANY A GLORIOUS MORNING HAVE I SEEN"

Full many a glorious morning have I seen
Flatter the mountain-tops with sovereign eye,
Kissing with golden face the meadows green,
Gilding pale streams with heavenly alchemy;
Anon permit the basest clouds to ride
With ugly wrack on his celestial face,
And from the forlorn world his visage hide,
Stealing unseen to west with foul disgrace:
Even so my sun one early morn did shine
With all-triumphant splendour on my brow;
But out, alack! he was but one hour mine,
The region cloud hath masked him from me now.
Yet him for this my love no whit disdaineth;
Suns of the world may stain when heaven's sun staineth.

William Shakespeare.

BALLADE OF GOOD COUNSEL

Flee fro the prees, and dwell with sothfastnessè;
Suffice unto thy thyng though hit be smal;
For hord hath hate and clymbyng tikelnessè,
Prees hath envỳe, and welè blent overal;
Savoùr no more than thee bihovè shal;
Werke wel thy-self, that other folk canst redè,
And trouthè shall deliverè, it is no dredè.

Tempèst thee noght al croked to redressè
In trust of hir that turneth as a bal:
Greet restè stant in litel besynessè;
And eek be war to sporne ageyn an al;

Stryve noght, as doth the crokkè with the wal.
Dauntè thy-self, that dauntest otherès dedè,
And trouthè shall delivere, it is no dredè.

That thee is sent, receyve in buxumnessè,
The wrastling for this world axeth a fal.
Her nis non hoom, her nis but wildernessè.
Forth, pilgrim, forth! Forth, beste, out of thy stal,
Know thy contrée, look up, thank God of al;
Holde the hye wey, and lat thy gost thee ledè,
And trouthè shall delivere, it is no dredè.

Envoy

Therfore, thou vache, leve thyn old wrecchednessè,
Unto the world; leve now to be a thral;
Crye him mercý, that of his hy goodnessè
Made thee of noght, and in especïal
Draw unto him, and pray in general
For thee, and eek for other, hevenlich medè;
And trouthè shall delivere, it is no dredè.

Geoffrey Chaucer.

FREEDOM

This is an extract from a very long poem on Robert the Bruce, which was written almost within the lifetime of the king by John Barbour, Archdeacon of Aberdeen. As they were composed in Scotland nearly six hundred years ago, it is not surprising that the language of these lines differs greatly from modern English. Chaucer's "Ballade of Good Counsel," which dates from the same time, and which contains the words of a Londoner, is equally strange and archaic, though in a different way.

Seeing that John Barbour lived during the Scottish War of Independence, and must often have talked with men who fought at Bannockburn, the priceless blessing of liberty meant a very great deal to him.

>   A! FREDOME is a noble thing!
>   Fredome mays man to haiff liking;
>   Fredome all solace to man giffis,
>   He levys at es that frely levys;
>   A noble hart may haiff nane es,
>   Na ellys nocht that may him ples,
>   Gyff fredome failth; for fre liking
>   Is yharnit our all other thing.
>   Na he that ay has levyt fre
>   May nocht knaw weill the propyrté,
>   The angyr, na the wretchyt dome
>   That is cowplyt to foule thraldome.
>   Bot gyff he had assayit it,
>   Than all perquer he suld it wit;
>   And suld think fredome mar to prys
>   Than all the gold in warld that is.
>   *John Barbour.*

"IT IS NOT TO BE THOUGHT OF THAT THE FLOOD"

IT is not to be thought of that the Flood
Of British freedom, which, to the open sea
Of the world's praise, from dark antiquity
Hath flowed, with pomp of waters, unwithstood,
Roused though it be full often to a mood
Which spurns the check of salutary bands,—
That this most famous Stream in bogs and sands
Should perish, and to evil and to good

Be lost for ever. In our halls is hung
Armoury of the invincible knights of old:
We must be free or die, who speak the tongue
That Shakespeare spake, the faith and morals hold
Which Milton held. In everything we are sprung
Of earth's first blood, have titles manifold.
                                    William Wordsworth.

ENGLAND AND SWITZERLAND, 1802

This sonnet was written when the liberty of England was threatened by the growing power of Napoleon. It shows that Poetry can deal with any idea—for Freedom might seem to be a subject fit only for an essay or a treatise—and by its vivid imagery and its inspiring tones can compress into a few lines as much force as would be contained in many prose volumes.

Two Voices are there: one is of the Sea,
One of the Mountains; each a mighty voice:
In both from age to age thou didst rejoice,
They were thy chosen music, Liberty!
There came a tyrant, and with holy glee
Thou fought'st against him, but hast vainly striven:
Thou from thy Alpine holds at length art driven,
Where not a torrent murmurs heard by thee.
Of one deep bliss thine ear hath been bereft;
Then cleave, O cleave to that which still is left:
For, high-souled maid, what sorrow would it be
That Mountain floods should thunder as before,
And Ocean bellow from his rocky shore,
And neither awful Voice be heard by Thee!
                                    William Wordsworth.

"THE WORLD IS TOO MUCH WITH US"

Besides this sonnet there are other poems in this volume which are expressions of the belief that man, to become truly good, and to remain truly good, must maintain communion with the spirit of Nature, and that it is at the peril of his soul that he severs the connexion by attending exclusively to human affairs. The preceding sonnet embodies the notion in a different form; there the love of liberty exhibited by nations living among mountains or near to the sea is attributed to the influence of their surroundings. In the ode on "The Intimations of Immortality" the same idea also plays a part.

THE world is too much with us; late and soon,
Getting and spending, we lay waste our powers;
Little we see in Nature that is ours;
We have given our hearts away, a sordid boon.
This Sea that bares her bosom to the moon,
The winds that will be howling at all hours,
And are upgathered now like sleeping flowers,—
For this, for everything, we are out of tune;
It moves us not. Great God! I'd rather be
A pagan suckled in a creed outworn,
So might I, standing on this pleasant lea,
Have glimpses that would make me less forlorn;
Have sight of Proteus rising from the sea;
Or hear old Triton blow his wreathèd horn.

William Wordsworth.

"MY MIND TO ME A KINGDOM IS"

My mind to me a kingdom is;
Such present joys therein I find
That it excels all other bliss
That earth affords or grows by kind:
Though much I want which most would have,
Yet still my mind forbids to crave.

No princely pomp, no wealthy store,
No force to win the victory,
No wily wit to salve a sore,
No shape to feed a loving eye:
To none of these I yield as thrall:
For why?—my mind doth serve for all.

I see how plenty surfeits oft,
And hasty climbers soon do fall;
I see that those which are aloft
Mishap doth threaten most of all:
They get with toil, they keep with fear:
Such cares my mind could never bear.

Some have too much, yet still do crave;
I little have, and seek no more.
They are but poor though much they have,
And I am rich with little store;
They poor, I rich; they beg, I give;
They lack, I leave; they pine, I live.

I laugh not at another's loss,
I grudge not at another's gain;
No worldly waves my mind can toss,
My state at one doth still remain;
I fear no foe, I fawn no friend;
I loathe not life nor dread my end.

Some weigh their pleasure by their lust,
Their wisdom by their rage of will;
Their treasure is their only trust,
A cloakèd craft their store of skill.
But all the pleasure that I find
Is to maintain a quiet mind.

My wealth is health and perfect ease;
My conscience clear my choice defence:
I neither seek by bribes to please,
Nor by deceit to breed offence;
Thus do I live, thus will I die:
Would all did so as well as I.

Sir Edward Dyer.

"HE THAT OF SUCH A HEIGHT HATH BUILT HIS MIND"

He that of such a height hath built his mind,
And reared the dwelling of his thoughts so strong,
As neither fear nor hope can shake the frame
Of his resolvèd powers : nor all the wind
Of vanity or malice pierce to wrong
His settled peace, or to disturb the same—
What a fair seat hath he, from whence he may
The boundless wastes and wealds of man survey!

And with how free an eye doth he look down
Upon these lower regions of turmoil,
Where all the storms of passion mainly [1] beat
On flesh and blood : where honour, power, renown,
Are only gay afflictions, golden toil :
Where greatness stands upon as feeble feet
As frailty doth, and only great doth seem
To little minds, who do it so esteem!

Samuel Daniel.

[1] Strongly.

THE CHAMBERED NAUTILUS

This is the ship of pearl which, poets feign,
    Sails the unshadowed main,—
    The venturous bark that flings
On the sweet summer wind its purpled wings
In gulfs enchanted, where the Siren sings,
    And coral-reefs lie bare,
Where the cold sea-maids rise to sun their streaming hair.

Its webs of living gauze no more unfurl;
    Wrecked is the ship of pearl.
    And every chambered cell,
Where its dim dreaming life was wont to dwell,
As the frail tenant shaped his growing shell,
    Before thee lies revealed,—
Its irised ceiling rent, its sunless crypt revealed.

Year after year beheld the silent toil
    That spread his lustrous coil;
    Still, as the spiral grew,
He left the past year's dwelling for the new,
Stole with soft step its shining archway through,
    Built up its idle door,
Stretched in his last-found home, and knew the old no more.

Thanks for the heavenly message brought by thee,
    Child of the wandering sea,
    Cast from her lap, forlorn!
From thy dead lips a clearer note is borne
Than ever Triton blew from wreathèd horn.
    While on mine ear it rings,
Through the deep caves of thought I hear a voice that sings :—

"Build thee more stately mansions, O my soul,
  As the swift seasons roll!
  Leave thy low-vaulted past!
Let each new temple, nobler than the last,
Shut thee from heaven with a dome more vast,
  Till thou at length art free,
Leaving thine outgrown shell by life's unresting sea!"

Oliver Wendell Holmes.

INTIMATIONS OF IMMORTALITY

The Greek philosopher Plato taught that the nature of man's mind proves that he has memories of a previous existence, that he has lived before this present life. In this ode Wordsworth used this idea, and added to it his own poetic belief that in youth we are more in contact with the spirit of Nature than when the business of life occupies our faculties and absorbs our attention. The poem contains a number of magnificent and most impressive phrases.

THERE was a time when meadow, grove, and stream,
The earth, and every common sight
  To me did seem
    Apparelled in celestial light,
The glory and the freshness of a dream.
It is not now as it hath been of yore, —
    Turn wheresoe'er I may,
    By night or day,
The things which I have seen I now can see no more.

  The rainbow comes and goes,
  And lovely is the rose;

The moon doth with delight
Look round her when the heavens are bare;
Waters on a starry night
Are beautiful and fair;
The sunshine is a glorious birth;
But yet I know, where'er I go,
That there hath passed away a glory from the earth.

Now, while the birds thus sing a joyous song,
And while the young lambs bound,
As to the tabor's sound,
To me alone there came a thought of grief:
A timely utterance gave that thought relief,
And I again am strong:
The cataracts blow their trumpets from the steep,
No more shall grief of mine the season wrong;
I hear the echoes through the mountains throng,
The winds come to me from the fields of sleep,
And all the earth is gay;
Land and sea
Give themselves up to jollity,
And with the heart of May
Doth every heart keep holiday:—
Thou child of joy,
Shout round me; let me hear thy shouts, thou happy shepherd boy!

Our birth is but a sleep and a forgetting:
The soul that rises with us, our life's star,
Hath had elsewhere its setting,
And cometh from afar:
Not in entire forgetfulness,
And not in utter nakedness,

Intimations of Immortality

But trailing clouds of glory do we come
    From God, who is our home.
Heaven lies about us in our infancy.
Shades of the prison-house begin to close
    Upon the growing boy;
But he beholds the light, and whence it flows;
    He sees it daily in his joy.
The youth, who daily farther from the east
    Must travel, still is Nature's priest;
      And by the vision splendid
      Is on his way attended.
At length the man perceives it die away,
And fade into the light of common day.

Earth fills her lap with pleasures of her own;
Yearnings she hath in her own natural kind,
And, even with something of a mother's mind,
    And no unworthy aim,
    The homely nurse doth all she can
    To make her foster-child, her inmate man,
    Forget the glories he hath known,
And that imperial palace whence he came.

    O joy, that in our embers
    Is something that doth live!
    That nature yet remembers
    What was so fugitive!
The thought of our past years in me doth breed
Perpetual benediction; not indeed
For that which is most worthy to be blest—
Delight and liberty, the simple creed
Of Childhood, whether busy or at rest,
With new-fledged hope still fluttering in his
    breast;

    Not for these I raise
    The song of thanks and praise,
  But for those obstinate questionings
  Of sense and outward things;
  Fallings from us, vanishings;
  Blank misgivings of a creature
Moving about in worlds not realised;
High instincts, before which our mortal nature
Did tremble like a guilty thing surprised:
    But for those first affections,
    Those shadowy recollections,
   Which, be they what they may,
Are yet the fountain-light of all our day,
Are yet a master-light of all our seeing;
Uphold us, cherish, and have power to make
Our noisy years seem moments in the being
Of the eternal silence :—truths that wake
    To perish never;
Which neither listlessness, nor mad endeavour,
    Nor man, nor boy,
Nor all that is at enmity with joy
Can utterly abolish and destroy.
    Hence, in a season of calm weather,
    Though inland far we be,
Our souls have sight of that immortal sea
    Which brought us hither,
    Can in a moment travel thither,
And see the children sport upon the shore,
And hear the mighty waters rolling evermore.

And, O ye fountains, meadows, hills, and groves,
Forbode not any severing of our loves!
Yet in my heart of hearts I feel your might:
I only have relinquished one delight

Intimations of Immortality

To live beneath your more habitual sway.
I love the brooks which down their channels fret
Even more than when I tripped lightly as they;
The innocent brightness of a new-born day
    Is lovely yet;
The clouds that gather round the setting sun
Do take a sober colouring from an eye
That hath kept watch o'er man's mortality;
Another race hath been, and other palms are won.
Thanks to the human heart by which we live,
Thanks to its tenderness, its joys, and fears,
To me the meanest flower that blows can give
Thoughts that do often lie too deep for tears.

   From " Intimations of Immortality,"
           by William Wordsworth.

CHORUS

Before the beginning of years
    There came to the making of man
Time, with a gift of tears;
    Grief, with a glass that ran;
Pleasure, with pain for leaven;
    Summer, with flowers that fell;
Remembrance fallen from heaven,
    And madness risen from hell;
Strength without hands to smite;
    Love that endures for a breath;
Night, the shadow of light;
    And life, the shadow of death.

And the high gods took in hand
    Fire, and the falling of tears,
And a measure of sliding sand
    From under the feet of the years;

And froth and drift of the sea;
  And dust of the labouring earth;
And bodies of things to be
  In the houses of death and of birth;
And wrought with weeping and laughter,
  And fashioned with loathing and love,
With life before and after
  And death beneath and above,
For a day and a night and a morrow,
  That his strength might endure for a span
With travail and heavy sorrow,
  The holy spirit of man.

From the winds of the north and the south
  They gathered as unto strife;
They breathed upon his mouth,
  They filled his body with life;
Eyesight and speech they wrought
  For the veils of the soul therein,
A time for labour and thought,
  A time to serve and to sin:
They gave him light in his ways,
  And love, and a space for delight,
And beauty and length of days,
  And night, and sleep in the night.
His speech is a burning fire;
  With his lips he travaileth;
In his heart is a blind desire,
  In his eyes foreknowledge of death;
He weaves, and is clothed with derision;
  Sows, and he shall not reap;
His life is a watch or a vision
  Between a sleep and a sleep.
From " Atalanta in Calydon," by
              Algernon Charles Swinburne.

"LIKE TO THE FALLING OF A STAR"

Like to the falling of a star;
Or as the flights of eagles are;
Or like the fresh spring's gaudy hue;
Or silver drops of morning dew;
Or like a wind that chafes the flood;
Or bubbles which on water stood—
Even such is man, whose borrowed light
Is straight called in, and paid to-night.
The wind blows out; the bubble dies;
The spring entombed in autumn lies;
The dew dries up; the star is shot;
The flight is past—and man forgot.
Bishop Henry King.

CHARLES THE TWELFTH

Even from his earliest boyhood, Charles XII, King of Sweden, was consumed by an insatiable thirst for military glory, and formed the desire to imitate Alexander the Great by conquering the world. His history is sufficiently related in the lines of stately verse which follow. He made war upon all the nations around him; he invaded Russia and penetrated to the centre. At first he was brilliantly successful, but after years of strife was utterly and finally defeated by Peter the Great at Pultowa in 1709. While inspecting trenches one night during the siege of a Norwegian fortress he was killed by a chance shot.

On what foundations stands the warrior's pride,
How just his hopes, let Swedish Charles decide.
A frame of adamant, a soul of fire,
No dangers fright him, and no labours tire;
O'er love, o'er fear, extends his wide domain,
Unconquered lord of pleasure and of pain;

No joys to him pacific sceptres yield,
War sounds the trump, he rushes to the field.
Behold surrounding kings their powers combine—
And one capitulate, and one resign:
Peace courts his hand, but spreads her charms in vain;
"Think nothing gained," he cries, "till nought remain;
On Moscow's walls till Gothic standards fly,
And all be mine beneath the Polar sky."

The march begins, in military state,
And nations on his eye suspended wait;
Stern Famine guards the solitary coast,
And Winter barricades the realms of frost.
He comes; nor want nor cold his course delay—
Hide, blushing Glory, hide Pultowa's day!

The vanquished hero leaves his broken bands,
And shows his miseries in distant lands,
Condemned a needy supplicant to wait,
While ladies interpose and slaves debate.
But did not Chance at length her error mend?
Did no subverted empire mark his end?
Did rival monarchs give the fatal wound?
Or hostile millions press him to the ground?—
His fall was destined to a barren strand,
A petty fortress, and a dubious hand.
He left the name at which the world grew pale
To point a moral, or adorn a tale.

From "The Vanity of Human Wishes,"
by Samuel Johnson.

RECESSIONAL

God of our fathers, known of old,
   Lord of our far-flung battle-lines,
Beneath whose awful Hand we hold
   Dominion over palm and pine—
Lord God of Hosts, be with us yet,
Lest we forget—lest we forget!

The tumult and the shouting dies;
   The captains and the kings depart;
Still stands Thine ancient sacrifice,
   An humble and a contrite heart.
Lord God of Hosts, be with us yet,
Lest we forget—lest we forget!

Far-called, our navies melt away;
   On dune and headland sinks the fire:
Lo, all our pomp of yesterday
   Is one with Nineveh and Tyre!
Judge of the nations, spare us yet,
Lest we forget—lest we forget!

If, drunk with sight of power, we loose
   Wild tongues that have not Thee in awe,
Such boastings as the Gentiles use,
   Or lesser breeds without the Law—
Lord God of Hosts, be with us yet,
Lest we forget—lest we forget!

For heathen heart that puts her trust
   In reeking tube and iron shard,
All valiant dust that builds on dust,
   And, guarding, calls not Thee to guard,

For frantic boast and foolish word—
Thy mercy on Thy people, Lord !
Rudyard Kipling.

THE CONCLUSION

Found in Sir Walter Raleigh's Bible, this little poem is said to have been written the night before his death.

Even such is Time, that takes in trust,
  Our youth, our joys, our all we have,
And pays us but with earth and dust ;
  Who, in the dark and silent grave,
  When we have wandered all our ways,
  Shuts up the story of our days.
But from this earth, this grave, this dust,
My God shall raise me up, I trust.
Sir Walter Raleigh.

"THE GLORIES OF OUR BLOOD AND STATE"

The glories of our blood and state
  Are shadows, not substantial things ;
There is no armour against Fate ;
  Death lays his icy hands on kings.
    Sceptre and Crown
    Must tumble down,
And in the dust be equal made
With the poor crooked scythe and spade.

Some men with swords may reap the field,
  And plant fresh laurels where they kill :
But their strong nerves at last must yield ;
  They tame but one another still :
    Early or late
    They stoop to fate,

"The glories of our blood and state" 137

And must give up their murmuring breath,
When they, poor captives, creep to death.

The garlands wither on your brow;
  Then boast no more your mighty deeds!
Upon Death's purple altar now
  See where the victor-victim bleeds.
    Your heads must come
    To the cold tomb:
Only the actions of the just
Smell sweet and blossom in their dust.
                    James Shirley.

UXBRIDGE ROAD

The Western Road goes streaming out to seek the cleanly wild,
It pours the city's dim desires towards the undefiled,
It sweeps betwixt the huddled homes about its eddies grown
To smear the little space between the city and the sown:
The torments of that seething tide who is there that can see?
There's one who walked with starry feet the western road by me!

He is the Drover of the soul; he leads the flock of men
All wistful on that weary track, and brings them back again.
The dreaming few, the slaving crew, the motley caste of life—
The wastrel and artificer, the harlot and the wife—

They may not rest, for ever pressed by one they
    cannot see ;
The one who walked with starry feet the western
    road by me.

He drives them east, he drives them west, between
    the dark and light ;
He pastures them in city pens, he leads them
    home at night.
The towery trams, the threaded trains, like
    shuttles to and fro
To weave the web of working days in ceaseless
    travel go.
How harsh the woof, how long the weft ! who
    shall the fabric see ?
The one who walked with starry feet the western
    road by me !

Throughout the living joyful year at lifeless tasks
    to strive,
And scarcely at the end to save gentility alive ;
The villa plot to sow and reap, to act the villa lie,
Beset by villa fears to live, midst villa dreams to
    die ;
Ah, who can know the dreary woe ? and who the
    splendour see ?
The one who walked with starry feet the western
    road by me.

Behold ! he lent me as we went the vision of the
    seer ;
Behold ! I saw the life of men, the life of God
    shine clear.

I saw the hidden Spirit's thrust; I saw the race
   fulfil
The spiral of its steep ascent, predestined of the
   will,
Yet not unled, but shepherded by one they may
   not see—
The one who walked with starry feet the western
   road by me !

      Evelyn Underhill.

ON HIS BLINDNESS

When I consider how my light is spent
Ere half my days, in this dark world and wide,
And that one talent which is death to hide
Lodged with me useless, though my soul more
   bent
To serve therewith my Maker, and present
My true account, lest He returning chide,—
" Doth God exact day-labour, light denied ? "
I fondly ask. But Patience, to prevent
That murmur, soon replies, " God doth not need
Either man's work, or His own gifts; who best
Bear His mild yoke, they serve Him best; His
   state
Is kingly; thousands at His bidding speed,
And post o'er land and ocean without rest;
They also serve who only stand and wait ! "

      John Milton.

THE BOOK

Of this fair volume which we " World " do name,
If we the sheets and leaves could turn with care,

Of Him who it corrects and did it frame
We clear might read the art and wisdom rare
Find out, His power which wildest powers doth
    tame,
His providence extending everywhere,
His justice which proud rebels doth not spare,
In every page, no period of the same.
But silly we, like foolish children, rest
Well pleased with coloured vellum, leaves of gold,
Fair dangling ribbands, leaving what is best,
On the great Writer's sense ne'er taking hold;
Or, if by chance we stay our minds on aught,
It is some picture on the margin wrought.

William Drummond.

ODE IN MAY

Let me go forth, and share
　　The overflowing Sun
　　With one wise friend, or one
Better than wise, being fair,
Where the peewit wheels and dips
　　On heights of bracken and ling,
And Earth, unto her leaflet tips,
　　Tingles with the Spring.

What is so sweet and dear
　　As a prosperous morn in May,
　　The confident prime of the day
And the dauntless youth of the year,
When nothing that asks for bliss,
　　Asking aright, is denied,
And half of the world a bridegroom is,
　　And half of the world a bride?

Ode in May

The Song of Mingling flows,
  Grave, ceremonial, pure,
  As once, from lips that endure,
The cosmic descant rose,
When the temporal lord of life,
  Going his golden way,
Had taken a wondrous maid to wife
  That long had said him nay.

For of old the Sun, our sire,
  Came wooing the mother of men,
  Earth, that was virginal then,
Vestal fire to his fire.
Silent her bosom and coy,
  But the strong god sued and pressed,
And born of their starry nuptial joy
  Are all that drink of her breast.

And the triumph of him that begot
  And the travail of her that bore,
  Behold, they are evermore
As warp and weft of our lot.
We are children of splendour and flame,
  Of shuddering, also, and tears;
Magnificent out of the dust we came,
  And abject from the spheres.

O bright irresistible lord!
  We are fruit of Earth's womb, each one.
  And fruit of thy love, O Sun,
For this thy spouse, thy adored.
To thee as our Father we bow,
  Forbidden thy Father to see,
Who is older and greater than thou, as thou
  Art greater and older than we.

Thou art but as a word of His speech,
   Thou art but as a wave of His hand;
   Thou art brief as a glitter of sand
'Twixt tide and tide on His beach;
Thou art less than a spark of His fire,
   Or a moment's mood of His soul:
Thou art lost in the notes on the lips of His choir
   That chant the chant of the whole.

Sir William Watson.

TO A SNOWFLAKE

What heart could have thought you?—
Past our devisal
(O filigree petal!)
Fashioned so purely,
Fragilely, surely,
From what Paradisal
Imagineless metal,
Too costly for cost?
Who hammered you, wrought you,
From argentine vapour?—
"God was my shaper.
Passing surmisal,
He hammered, He wrought me,
From curled silver vapour,
To lust of His mind:—
Thou couldst not have thought me!
So purely, so palely,
Tinily, surely,
Mightily, frailly,
Insculped and embossed,
With His hammer of wind,
And His graver of frost."

Francis Thompson.

"NIGHT UNTO NIGHT SHOWETH KNOWLEDGE"

When I survey the bright
    Celestial sphere ;
So rich with jewels hung, that Night
  Doth like an Ethiop bride appear :

My soul her wings doth spread
    And heavenward flies,
The Almighty's mysteries to read
  In the large volumes of the skies.

For the bright firmament
    Shoots forth no flame
So silent, but is eloquent
  In speaking the Creator's name.

No unregarded star
    Contracts its light
Into so small a character
  Removed far from our human sight,

But, if we steadfast look,
    We shall discern
In it, as in some holy book,
  How man may heavenly knowledge learn.

It tells the conqueror
    That far-stretched power,
Which his proud dangers[1] traffic for
  Is but the triumph of an hour :

That from the farthest North
    Some nation may,

[1] Armies

Yet undiscovered, issue forth,
    And o'er his new-got conquest sway:

Some nation yet shut in
    With hills of ice
May be let out to scourge his sin,
    Till they shall equal him in vice.

And then they likewise shall
    Their ruin have;
For as yourselves your empires fall,
    And every kingdom hath a grave.

Thus those celestial fires,
    Though seeming mute,
The fallacy of our desires
    And all the pride of life confute:—

For they have watched since first
    The world had birth:
And found sin in itself accurst,
    And nothing permanent on earth.
              William Habington.

VERSE EXERCISES

METRE

POETRY can be enjoyed without the manner in which it is constructed being understood; indeed, it is a mistake to pay too much attention to its structure. But the structure is not hard to understand, and, once gained and if properly used, the knowledge adds greatly to the enjoyment which poetry can give to the reader.

If the stressed syllables are marked in a piece of prose, it will be found that they occur irregularly, as in: " I have trávelled múch in the reálms of gold, and seén mány goódly státes and kíngdoms; I háve beén round mány wéstern íslands which bárds hóld in feälty to Apóllo." In this passage every word of more than one syllable contains a syllable that is stronger than the rest, and some of the monosyllabic words are emphasized more than the others.

Very different is the effect of the same words if they are arranged as the author wrote them:

> Múch have I trávelled ìn the reálms of góld,
> And mány goódly státes and kíngdoms seén;
> Round mány wéstern íslands hàve I beén
> Which bárds in feälty tò Apóllo hóld.

The poetical expressions which the original sentences contained are now placed in a fit setting, so that their beauty shines forth gloriously. The reason is that a rhythm has been produced by the regular arrangement of the stressed syllables. So strong is the effect of this regular arrangement, which is called the *metre*, that some syllables that in the first sentence had no accent have now been endowed with one—weak, it is true, but distinctly perceptible.

Words which contain rhythm and metre are verse: without metre words and sentences, however beautiful and inspired, are not verse, and with metre, however mean they are in other respects, they are verse. Metre, which is the mechanical part of poetry, is perhaps not its most important characteristic, but it is essential; metre is the framework of the structure.

It is not to be supposed that the poet concentrates his attention upon the metre, when he is composing; he does not think of a regular alternation of syllables; he has a rhythm in his mind, which for the time has become natural to him; he cannot escape it, and upon the skill with which he writes it, conforms to it, varies it, depends in no small degree the beauty of his verse. At the moment of creation he cannot examine the metre. Afterwards he may examine it, and may make corrections and alterations at any points which jar upon his ear.

SCANSION

To comprehend the structure of poetry some means of describing metres is needed. This is obtained by discovering the manner in which the stressed and unstressed syllables are arranged, and then dividing the lines into pieces similar to one another, e.g. :

> My fáth|er léft | a párk | to mé,
> Bút it | is wíld | and bár|ren ;
> A gárd|en toó, | with scárce | a treé,
> And wást|er thàn | a wárr|en.

In this quatrain the first and third lines can be cut into four segments, each of which is called a *foot*, and each of which is similar to the rest. The second and fourth lines can be divided into three feet, together with an extra syllable. The feet are not real divisions in the verse—which is, of course, continuous at many places where the divisions are placed; they are merely the necessary device for describing the regular alternation of an unaccented with an accented syllable which is the basis of the rhythm in this poem.

In English poetry there are several kinds of feet which are frequently used. The commonest is that seen in the illustration just given, and is called an *iambus*. By far the greater part of English poetry is written in iambic metre. The reverse arrangement, that is, an accented syllable followed by an unaccented syllable, is called a *trochee*, e.g. :

Tíme and | chánce are | bút a | tíde ;
Slíghted | lóve is | sáir to | bíde.

There are no other kinds of two-syllabled feet, for every foot must contain an accent, and cannot contain two accents. In feet of three syllables, the stress may be on the first syllable (*dactyl*), on the middle syllable (*amphibrach*), or on the last (*anapaest*). There is no need to make use of one-syllabled feet, or of feet of more than three syllables. All ordinary verse can be described by means of these five kinds of feet, and, though exceptional lines occur, they can all be reduced to these terms, with the exercise of a little ingenuity.

Examples of verse written in these metres are :

(1) *Dactyls*.

Stíll stands the | fórest pri|méval ; but | únder the | sháde of its | bránches ,
Dwélls an|óther | ráce, with | óther | cústoms and | lánguage ;
Ónly a|lóng the | shóre of the | moúrnful and | místy At|lántic
Línger a | féw Ac|ádian | peásants, whose | fáthers from | éxile
Wándered | báck to their | nátive | lánd to | díe in its | bósom.

(2) *Amphibrachs.*

Knów ye | the lánd where | the cýpress | and mýrtle
Are émblems | of deéds that | are dóne in | their clíme ?
Where the ráge of | the vúlture, | the lóve of | the túrtle,
Now mélt in|to sórrow, | now mádden | to críme ?

(3) *Anapaests.*

Then he róse | at ónce | to his feét, | and smóte | the hárp | with his hánd,
And it ráng | as íf | with a crý | in the dréam | of a lóne|ly lánd ;
Then he fónd|led its wáil | as it fád|ed, and órd|erly óv|er the stríngs
Went the már|vellous soúnd | of its swéet|*ness*, like the márch | of Ód|in's kíngs.

All these metres, as the preceding instances show, are written with many irregularities, which may be described as an extra unaccented syllable within the line, or at the beginning, or at the end ; the omission of an unaccented syllable anywhere ; and the irregular placing of accents. The metre must prevail: if the irregularities are too many, the effect is lost, and the verse deteriorates into prose. But much of the metrical beauty arises from the irregularities ; if the metre is too regular, the verse becomes monotonous.

RHYME, ALLITERATION, AND ASSONANCE

Since the beauty of verse lies to a very great extent in its sound, there are many ornaments connected with this, the chief being rhyme, alliteration, and assonance.

RHYME.—Two accented syllables are said to rhyme perfectly when, beginning with different sounds, they contain identical vowels, followed, if followed at all, by identical consonants, as *lie, sky; these, trees.* If there are any further syllables, these coincide, as in *weáther, togéther ; hóllow, swállow ; moúntain, foúntain,* which are double rhymes; and *sórrowing, bórrowing,* which are triple rhymes.

Many of the rhymes found in English poetry are not quite perfect, as *door, poor; home, come.*

Rhyme is generally used at the ends of the lines, and serves to mark the divisions of the verse as well as to beautify the sound: but it may occur within the lines, as in:

> Perchance the lion stalking
>   Still shuns that hallowed spot;
> For beast and *bird* have seen and *heard*
>   That which man knoweth not.

ALLITERATION consists of the repetition of the same consonant sound, as in:

> *B*ritannia *n*eeds *n*o *b*ulwarks,
>   No towers along the steep;
> Her *m*arch is o'er the *m*ountain waves,
>   Her home is on the deep.

ASSONANCE is vowel alliteration, that is, the repetition of the same vowel sound; it is much rarer than alliteration in English poetry. It is seen in:

> Above my h*ea*d the h*ea*ven,
> The s*ea* ben*ea*th my f*ee*t.

STANZAS

By means of their rhymes, lines of different kinds and lengths can be bound together in stanzas, of which there are a very large number. Thus, in:

> Fair stood the wind for France   (*a*)
> When we our sails advance,   (*a*)
> Nor now to prove our chance   (*a*)
>   Longer will tarry;   (*b*)
> But, putting to the main,   (*c*)
> At Caux, the mouth of Seine,   (*c*)
> With all his martial train   (*c*)
>   Landed King Harry   (*b*)

the first three lines have the same rhyme, while another rhyme joins the fifth, sixth, and seventh lines. To hold together the first and second halves of the stanza, the short lines—the fourth and eighth—are rhymed with a double rhyme. The scheme of the rhymes is shown by the lettering.

Among common stanzas are:

(1) Two lines of five iambic feet rhymed, and known as the Heroic Couplet, e.g.:

> Each change of many-coloured life he drew,
> Exhausted realms, and then invented new;

> Existence saw him spurn her bounded reign,
> And panting Time toiled after him in vain.

(2) Two lines of seven iambic feet rhymed, as in:

Attend, all ye who list to hear our noble England's praise;
I tell of the thrice-famous deeds she wrought in ancient days.

This is called the Ballad Stanza, and is usually printed as a quatrain of lines of four and three feet alternately, thus:

> Attend, all ye who list to hear
> Our noble England's praise;
> I tell of the thrice-famous deeds
> She wrought in ancient days.

(3) Seven five-foot iambic lines, rhymed *a, b, a, b, b, c, c,* are called Rhyme Royal, e.g.

In a far country that I cannot name,	(*a*)
And on a year long ages past away,	(*b*)
A king there dwelt, in rest and ease and fame,	(*a*)
And richer than the Emperor is to-day;	(*b*)
The very thought of what this man might say,	(*b*)

Verse Exercises

From dusk to dawn kept many a lord awake; (c)
For fear of him did many a great man quake. (c)

(4) A verse of eight lines of five iambic feet, followed by one line of six feet, the rhymes being arranged *a, b, a, b, b, c, b, c, c*, is termed a Spenserian Stanza: see pp. 76 and 77 for examples.

(5) A Sonnet is a poem of fourteen lines, each containing five iambic feet; the rhymes may be arranged in various ways. There are several sonnets in this book (on pp. 17, 41, 46, 91, 119, 121, 122, 123, and 139).

These are only a few of the most famous of English stanzas, and all of them are old. They are still used by modern poets, who, in addition, are accustomed to invent stanzas of their own. Examples of modern stanzas will be found on pp. 15, 49, 78, 83, 126, 131.

The following exercises are divided into two sets, A being simpler than B.

A

1. Scan (that is, mark the accents and divide into feet), adding the rhyme-scheme in each case:

   (*a*) Beside yon straggling fence that skirts the way,
   With blossomed furze unprofitably gay,
   There, in his noisy mansion, skilled to rule,
   The village master taught his little school.

   (*b*) O, first he sang a merry song,
   And then he sang a grave:
   And then he pecked his feathers gray,
   To her the letter gave.

   (*c*) As I went down the water side,
   None but my foe to be my guide,
   None but my foe to be my guide
   On fair Kirconnel lea.

(d) Behold her, single in the field,
Yon solitary Highland lass!
Reaping and singing by herself:
 Stop here or gently pass!
Alone she cuts and binds the grain,
And sings a melancholy strain;
Oh, listen! for the vale profound
Is overflowing with the sound.

(e) There I suck the liquid air,
All amidst the gardens fair
Of Hesperus, and his daughters three
That sing about the golden tree.

(f) It is the land that freemen till,
 That sober-suited Freedom chose;
 The land where, girt with friends or foes,
A man may speak the thing he will.

(g) The curfew tolls the knell of parting day,
 The lowing herd wind slowly o'er the lea,
The plowman homeward plods his weary way,
 And leaves the world to darkness and to me.

(h) Their heads all stooping low, their points all in a row,
Like a whirlwind on the trees, like a deluge on the dykes,
Our cuirassiers have burst on the ranks of the accurst,
And at a shock have scattered the forest of his pikes.

(i) My England, island England, such leagues and leagues away,
It's years since I was with thee, when April wanes to May:
Years since I saw the primrose, and watched the brown hillside
Put on white crowns of blossom, and blush like April's bride.

Verse Exercises

(*j*) It was roses, roses, all the way,
    With myrtle mixed in my path like mad:
The house-roofs seemed to heave and sway,
    The church-spires flamed, such flags they had,
A year ago on this very day.

(*k*) And steeples far away you'll spy through veils of mist that muffle them,
    Where old and scarred they rise and guard God's acre of dead souls;
And round them barley stems that bow as sudden breezes ruffle them,
And fairy fingers shuffle them
With every wave that rolls.

(*l*) The ewes and the lambs, with the kids and their dams,
    To see in the country how finely they play;
The bells they do ring, and the birds they do sing,
And the fields and the gardens are pleasant and gay.
O, the oak, and the ash, and the bonny ivy-tree,
Do flourish at home in my own countrie!

(*m*) I bring fresh showers for the thirsting flowers,
    From the seas and the streams;
I bear light shade for the leaves when laid
    In their noonday dreams.
From my wings are shaken the dews that waken
    The sweet birds every one,
When rocked to rest on their mother's breast,
    As she dances about the sun.
I wield the flail of the lashing hail,
    And whiten the green plains under,

154 A Book of English Poems

And then again I dissolve it in rain,
And laugh as I pass in thunder.

(*n*) The laird o' Cockpen, he's proud and he's great,
His mind is ta'en up with things o' the State;
He wanted a wife his braw hoose to keep,
But favour wi' wooin' was fashious to seek.

2. Replace the italicized compound words in these lines by simple words equivalent, or nearly equivalent, in meaning. Where it is impossible to do so, state the reason.

(*a*) The birds that sing on autumn eves
Among the *golden-tinted* leaves.

(*b*) Wanders the silver Thames along
His *hoary-winding* way.

(*c*) A jewel in a *ten-times-barred-up* chest.

(*d*) The grains of sand so *shining-small*
Soft through my fingers ran.

(*e*) And one, that clashed in arms,
By glimmering lanes and walls of canvas led,
Threading the *soldier-city*.

3. Invent a compound word for each of those italicized in:

(*a*) *Towered* cities please us then,
And the busy hum of men.

(*b*) Behold the *radiant* Spring,
In splendour decked anew.

(*c*) There is a hill beside the *silver* Thames
Shady with birch and beech and odorous pine.

(*d*) When the *rusty* blackbird strips,
Bunch by bunch, the coral thorn.

Verse Exercises

4. Read aloud, and then mark the stressed syllables in:

> He was a handsome young fellow, with a peculiarly pleasant and friendly look about his eyes—an expression which was quite new to me then, though I soon became familiar with it. For the rest, he was dark-haired and berry-brown of skin, well-knit and strong, and obviously used to exercising his muscles, but with nothing rough or coarse about him, and clean as might be. His dress was not like any modern work-a-day clothes I had seen, but would have served very well for a picture of fourteenth-century life: it was of dark-blue cloth, simple enough, but of fine web, and without a stain on it. He had a brown leather belt round his waist, and I noticed that its clasp was of damascened steel beautifully wrought.

5. Mark the accented syllables in:

> For Arthur on the Whitsuntide before
> Held court at old Caerleon-upon-Usk.
> There on a day, he sitting high in hall,
> Before him came a forester of Dean,
> Wet from the woods, with notice of a hart
> Taller than all his fellows, milky-white,
> First seen that day: these things he told the king.
> Then the good king gave order to let blow
> His horns for hunting on the morrow morn.

6. Mark the alliteration in:

> (*a*) The fair breeze blew, the white foam flew,
>   The furrow followed free;
>   We were the first that ever burst
>   Into that silent sea.
>
> (*b*) With many a curve my banks I fret,
>   By many a field and fallow,
>   And many a fairy foreland set
>   With willow-weed and mallow.

    (*c*)   The combat deepens. On, ye brave,
          Who rush to glory, or the grave!
          Wave, Munich, all thy banners wave,
          And charge with all thy chivalry!

7. Change the following similes into metaphors:
    (*a*)   And the sheen of their spears was *like stars on the sea*.
    (*b*)   And all around the snowy mountains swim *Like mighty swans afloat in heaven's pool*.
    (*c*)   Their heads all stooping low, their points all in a row,
          Like a whirlwind on the trees, like a deluge on the dykes,
          Our cuirassiers have burst on the ranks of the accurst.

8. Change the following metaphors into similes:
    (*a*)   *Much have I travelled in the realms of gold* (see p. 17).
    (*b*)   *Gather ye rosebuds* while ye may (see p. 3).
    (*c*)   While the bee, with honied thigh,
          That at her flowery work doth sing,
          And the waters murmuring. . . .
          Entice the *dewy-feathered* sleep (see p. 36).

9. Translate into Blank Verse:

O Lord, how manifold are thy works! in wisdom hast thou made them all. The earth is full of thy riches; so is this great and wide sea, wherein are things creeping innumerable, both small and great beasts. There go the ships; there is that great leviathan whom thou hast made to play therein. These all wait upon thee, that thou mayest give them their meat in due season. Thou hidest thy face, they are troubled; thou takest away their breath, they die, and return to their dust. Thou sendest forth thy

Verse Exercises

spirit, they are created; and thou renewest the face of the earth. The glory of the Lord shall endure for ever; the Lord shall rejoice in his works. He looketh on the earth, and it trembleth; he toucheth the hills, and they smoke. I will sing unto the Lord as long as I live; I will sing praise to my God while I have my being.

10. Complete the following stanzas, of which the first two lines and the rhyme scheme are given, by translating the prose parts into lines of the correct metre and length.

   (*a*) I loved the brimming wave that swam   (*a*)
   Through quiet meadows round the mill, (*b*)
   Above the weir there was a sleepy pool, and another below it which was always seething and troubled. (*a, b*)

   (*b*) At first on his left hand uprose   (*a*)
   Great cliffs and sheer, and rent from
       those,   (*b*)
   Huge rocks lay on the sand, making progress difficult and slow. (*a, b*)

   (*c*) But still as wilder blew the wind,   (–)
   And as the night grew drearer,   (*a*)
   The sound of armed men riding along the valley grew louder and louder. (–, *a*; in this example make an internal rhyme for line 3.)

   (*d*) St. Agnes Eve—ah, bitter cold it was! (*a*)
   The owl, for all his feathers, was a-cold; (*b*)
   The hare ran shivering through the snow, and the sheep cowered silently in their pens. (*a, b*)

   (*e*) I saw a cherry-tree in flower,   (*a*)
   All radiant from a passing shower   (*a*)
   It shone against the deep blue sky, and it was most beautiful. (*b, b*)

(j) Forget six counties overhung with smoke,(*a*)
Forget the snorting steam and piston
    stroke, (*a*)
Forget the spreading of the hideous town, (*b*)
  And think of wandering on the hills, and
dream that London is still a small clean city,
whose green gardens border the Thames.
(*b*, *c*, *c*)

B

1. Point out in what respects the poetical figures in these two passages illustrate and adorn their subjects:

    (*a*) Simile: SATAN FALLEN FROM HEAVEN.

                    He above the rest,
    In shape and gesture proudly eminent,
    Stood like a tower. His form had not yet lost
    All her original brightness, nor appeared
    Less than Archangel ruined, and the excess
    Of glory obscured. *As when the sun new-risen*
    Looks through the horizontal misty air
    Shorn of his beams, or, from behind the moon,
    In dim eclipse, disastrous twilight sheds
    On half the nations, darkened so yet shone
    Above them all the Archangel.

    (*b*) Personification: DEATH.

                        That shape,
    If shape it might be called that shape had none
    Distinguishable in member, joint, or limb,
    Or substance might be called that shadow seemed,
    For each seemed either—black it stood as night,

> Fierce as ten furies, terrible as hell,
> And shook a dreadful dart. What seemed his head
> The likeness of a kingly crown had on.

2. (*a*) Complete each stanza of the ensuing poem in a consistent manner, and then (*b*) change it into a comic poem by substituting an anticlimax for each of the lines you have added.

> When Mars, the god of war on high,
>   Of battles first did think,
> He girt his sword upon his thigh,
>   And......................
>
> But love drove battles from his head,
>   And sick of wounds and scars,
> To Venus bright he went and said,
>   ....
>
> Thus love compelled the god to yield,
>   And seek for purer joys:
> He laid aside his helm and shield,
>   And......................

3. Convert this piece of blank verse into rhymed couplets in the same metre:

A Winter Dawn

> 'Tis morning, and the sun, with ruddy orb
> Ascending, fires the horizon, while the clouds
> That crowd away before the rising wind,
> More ardent as the disc emerges more,
> Resemble most some city in a blaze,
> Seen through the leafless wood. His slanting ray
> Slides ineffectual down the snowy vale,
> And, tingeing all with his own rosy hue,
> From every herb and every spiry blade
> Stretches a length of shadow o'er the field.

4. This is a prose description of the same scene as forms the subject of the sonnet on p. 91. Compare the two, and show as completely as you can what is present in the poem which is absent from the prose extract:

"We left London on Saturday morning at half-past five or six, the 31st of July. We mounted the Dover Coach at Charing Cross. It was a beautiful morning. The City, St. Paul's, with the river, and a multitude of little boats, made a most beautiful sight as we crossed Westminster Bridge. The houses were not overhung by their cloud of smoke, and they were spread out endlessly, yet the sun shone so brightly, with such a fierce light, that there was even something like the purity of one of Nature's own grand spectacles."

5. Change the following passage of prose into stanzas of the same kind as those on pp. 90 and 91.

"Once, in an ancient city, there was an enchanted well, which had lain for centuries shrouded in darkness; for there was a legend that a terrible catastrophe would occur if it should be uncovered. At length some careless hand left open the door that had enclosed it, and the morning sunlight flashed upon its waters. Immediately it rose responsive to the beam; it burst the barriers that confined it; it submerged the city that had surrounded it; and its resistless waves, chanting wild music to heaven, rolled over the temples and the palaces of the past."

6. Convert this account of Robinson Crusoe's escape from drowning into stanzas like those on p. 70. (See the model given below.)

Verse Exercises

I

We had very good weather all the way till we were many days out from land. But then a violent storm took us quite out of our knowledge, and blew in such a terrible manner that for twelve days we could do nothing but drive. During these twelve days we expected every day to be swallowed by the sea.

Model:
Day after day our good ship sped
  Before the tempest's breath;
And fast we flew through storm and spray,
  Each man expecting death.

II

In this distress, one of our men, early in the morning, cried out "Land!" and in a moment the ship struck upon a sand, and, her motion being so stopped, the sea broke over her in such a manner that we thought we should all have perished immediately.

III

We knew not where we were, nor upon what land we were driven, but the men got a boat slung over the ship's side, and, getting into her, we let go, and committed ourselves to God's mercy, and the wild sea.

IV

As we made nearer the shore, the land looked more frightful than the sea. After we had been driven for about a league, a raging wave, mountain-like, came rolling upon us, and took us with such a fury that it overset the boat at once.

V

Though I could swim very well, yet I could not deliver myself from the water so as to draw breath. But that wave, having driven me a vast way on towards the land, and having spent itself, went back and left me upon the sand.

VI

So, getting upon my feet, I endeavoured to make towards the land as fast as I could, before another wave should return and take me up again. Then I saw the sea come after me as huge as a great hill, and as furious as an enemy.

VII

It buried me at once twenty or thirty feet deep in its own body, and I could feel myself carried with a mighty force and swiftness towards the shore a very great way, and at last I caught hold of a rock. Twice more was I thus lifted up by the waves.

VIII

At last, to my great comfort, I reached the land, clambered up the cliffs, and sat down upon the grass, quite out of the reach of the water. But I was scarce able to breathe for the sea-water I had drunk, and was very distressed in mind, for I was alone, all my companions having been lost in that terrible sea.

7. Translate into three stanzas of the same form as those on pp. 78 and 79:

My little bit of land is an untilled pebbly expanse, desolate, barren, sun-scorched, and overgrown with thistles. It is too poor to be worth

Verse Exercises

the trouble of ploughing; but the sheep pass there in spring, when it has chanced to rain and a little grass grows up. There are plenty of weeds; couch-grass and centaury, and the fierce Spanish oyster-plant, with its spreading orange flowers, and its spikes strong as nails. There are thistles, too, and well-armed prickly knapweeds; and, in among them, in long lines provided with hooks, the shoots of the blue dewberry creep along the ground.

This curious, barren Paradise is the happy hunting-ground of bees and wasps, and on hot summer afternoons you may see ants, who leave their barracks in long battalions, and march far afield to hunt for slaves.

8. From the following passage make a sonnet like that on pp. 17 and 18, or that on p. 119; the title of the sonnet will be "Truth."

Truth came into the world with her Divine Master, and was a perfect shape most glorious to look on; but when He ascended, and His Apostles after Him were laid asleep, then straight arose a wicked race of deceivers, who took the virgin Truth, hewed her lovely form into a thousand pieces, and scattered them to the four winds. From that time since, the sad friends of Truth, such as durst appear, went up and down gathering up limb by limb still as they could find them. We have not yet found them all, nor ever shall do till her Master's Second Coming; He shall bring together every joint and member, and shall mould them into an immortal feature of loveliness and perfection.

Brewer's Handbook of
English Literature

Ode — a poem that can be sung
Sonnet — a " of 14 lines
Ballad — a little song.
Epic — a poem containing heroic narrat[ive]
Lyric (1) " " written in stanzas
Narrative Poem (2) a story relating particul[ar]
Pastoral " — a poem describing rural lif[e]
Nature " (3)

dialect — a poem written in local form
of speech

P. 62 — Metaphors & Simile

Notes by M. Nathaniel, B.A.